SPECTRUM®

Take the mystery out of the Common Core State Standards and help your child succeed!

Schools in most U.S. states have adopted Common Core State Standards for English Language Arts and Mathematics, raising the bar for student achievement.

What are these new learning standards, and how can you help your child succeed in today's standards-based classroom? Discover the answers inside *Spectrum Language Arts and Math: Common Core Edition*. This parent-friendly workbook provides all the resources you need to support your child's learning at school this year.

Resources in this book include:

- An easy-to-understand explanation for each Common Core standard in ~~~~~~~~~ el

- Plenty of practice activities so your child can review and improve each Common Core skill

- Fun extension activities for helping your child at home

- Over 100 learning cards for more skill-building practice

LEARNING SPOT™

Visit
learningspotlibrary.com
for FREE activities!

CARSON-DELLOSA™
PUBLISHING GROUP

P.O. Box 35665 • Greensboro, NC 27425 USA

carsondellosa.com

U.S. $12.99
ISBN-13: 978-1-4838-0598-6
51299

EAN
9 781483 805986

Stop the summer slide.
Start Summer Bridge Activities®.

You've probably heard of "summer learning loss," or the "summer slide." Studies have shown that children can *lose up to 2.5 months of learning* over the summer. But did you know that summer learning loss could have a cumulative effect with a long-term impact on children's skills and success?

Summer Bridge Activities® are an easy, effective and fun way to keep your child's mind sharp all summer long.

Inside each book you'll find:

* Essential math, language arts, reading, social studies, science, and character development skills

* Encouraging stickers and certificates to keep kids motivated

* ...ies to keep them moving

* ...mmer Bridge Activities® online companion site

...ties®, your child will be on track for a terrific school year, and beyond.
...inutes a day goes a long way!*

Newly updated, *Summer Bridge Activities®* books align to the Common Core and state standards.

carsondellosa.com/summerbridge

SPECTRUM®
Common Core Edition
Language Arts
and Math

Published by Spectrum®
An imprint of Carson-Dellosa Publishing LLC
Greensboro, North Carolina

Spectrum®
An imprint of Carson-Dellosa Publishing LLC
P.O. Box 35665
Greensboro, NC 27425 USA

    ISBN 978-1-4838-0598-6

01-046157811

Table of Contents

Introduction to the Common Core State Standards
Grade 2

Why Are Common Core State Standards Important for My Child?

The Common Core State Standards are a set of guidelines that outline what children are expected to learn at school. Most U.S. states have voluntarily adopted the standards. Teachers, principals, and administrators in these states use the standards as a blueprint for classroom lessons, district curriculum, and statewide tests. The standards were developed by a state-led collaboration between the Council of Chief State School Officers (CCSSO) and the National Governors Association (NGA).

The Common Core Standards set high expectations for your child's learning. They are up-to-date with 21st century technology and draw on the best practices of excellent schools around the world. They focus on important skills in reading, language arts, and math. Common Core State Standards aim to ensure that your child will be college and career ready by the end of high school and able to compete in our global world.

What Are the Common Core State Standards for My Second Grade Student?
Common Core State Standards for your second grader are designed to build a solid foundation for reading, literacy, and mathematical understanding. On practice pages in this book, you will find references to specific Common Core Standards that teachers will expect your child to know by the end of the year. Completing activities on these pages will help your child master essential skills for success in second grade.

A Sample of Common Core Language Arts Skills for Grade 2*
- Read a fable or folktale and determine the moral of the story.
- Make connections between ideas in a nonfiction article about history, science, or technology.
- Think about the reasons an author gives to back up points.
- Know how to spell words with short vowel and long vowel sounds.
- Write to give opinions, provide information, and tell stories.
- Capitalize names of people, places, and things.
- Use a dictionary to find word meanings and spellings.

A Sample of Common Core Math Skills for Grade 2*
- Distinguish between odd and even numbers.
- Use addition and subtraction to solve word problems within 100.
- Skip-count by 5s, 10s, and 100s.
- Mentally add 10 or 100 to a given number.
- Estimate lengths in inches, feet, centimeters, and meters.
- Solve word problems about money amounts.
- Work with picture graphs and bar graphs.

How to Use This Book
In this book, you will find a complete **Common Core State Standards Overview** for second grade English Language Arts (pages 6–9) and Math (pages 64–67). Read these pages to learn more about the Common Core Standards and what you can expect your child to learn at school this year.

Then, choose **Practice Pages** that best address your child's needs for building skills that meet specific standards. Help your child complete practice pages and check the answers.

Finally, assist your child in cutting apart the **Flash Cards** found at the back of the book. These handy cards, which provide even more practice with Common Core skills, are suitable for use at home or on the go.

At the bottom of each practice page, you will find a **Helping at Home** tip that provides fun and creative ideas for additional practice with the skill at home.

Common Core State Standards for English Language Arts*

The following parent-friendly explanations of second grade Common Core English language arts standards are provided to help you understand what your child will learn in school this year. Practice pages listed will help your child master each skill.

Complete Common Core State Standards may be found here: www.corestandards.org.

RL/RI.2 Reading Standards for Literature and Informational Text

Key Ideas and Details
(Standards: RL.2.1, RL.2.2, RL.2.3, RI.2.1, RI.2.2, RI.2.3)

After reading a story or information article, your child will ask and answer who, what, where, when, why, and how questions about details from the text.
• **Practice pages: 10, 11, 15, 16, 20, 23–26, 28–30**

After reading a story, your child will describe the message or moral of the story. After reading an information article, your child will describe its main topic. • **Practice pages: 12, 21–24**

Your child will discuss events that happen in a story and think about how the characters respond. For example, your child will think about the events that lead Jack to sell his cow for magic beans in "Jack and the Beanstalk." • **Practice page: 13**

When reading nonfiction articles, your child will make connections between historical events, scientific ideas, or steps in a process. For example, he or she might describe how each step leads to the next when reading about the water cycle. • **Practice page: 22**

Craft and Structure
(Standards: RL.2.4, RL.2.5, RL.2.6, RI.2.4, RI.2.5, RI.2.6)

When reading stories, poems, and song lyrics, your child will point out words and phrases that create repetition, rhythm, and rhyme. • **Practice page: 14**

When your child comes to an unknown word, he or she will search the surrounding text for clues to its meaning. • **Practice pages: 23, 24, 59**

Your child will think about the basic structure of a story and understand that the action is introduced during a story's beginning and concludes during a story's ending.
• **Practice page: 15**

Your child will learn the habit of using features such as bold type, headings, and menus to locate information. • **Practice pages: 23–26**

When reading a story, your child will think about different points of view and use a different voice for each character when reading dialogue aloud. • **Practice pages: 12, 15, 16**

When reading, your child will think about the author's purpose. He or she will ask, "What is this author trying to answer, explain, or describe?" • **Practice page: 27**

Integration of Knowledge and Skills
(Standards: RL.2.7, RL.2.9, RI.2.7, RI.2.8, RI.2.9)

Your child will look at illustrations, charts, and diagrams and ask, "How does this help me understand what I am reading?" • **Practice pages: 19, 25, 26**

When reading a nonfiction article, your child will look for reasons and evidence an author uses to back up points. • **Practice page: 28**

Your child will read two similar stories or two nonfiction articles about the same topic and think about how they are alike and different. • **Practice pages: 17, 18, 29, 30**

RF.2 Reading Standards: Foundational Skills

Phonics and Word Recognition
(Standards: RF.2.3a, RF.2.3b, RF.2.3c, RF.2.3d, RF.2.3e, RF.2.3f)

When reading simple words such as cap and cape, your child will tell which have short vowel sounds (as in cap) and which have long vowel sounds (as in cape). He or she will tell which letters spell the vowel sound in each word. • **Practice pages: 31, 32, 35**

Your child will learn that combinations of vowel letters, or "vowel teams," are often used in words such as boat, wait, coin, and feet to spell long vowel sounds. • **Practice pages: 33, 34**

Your child will count syllables in longer words he or she is reading and recognize that each syllable contains a vowel sound. • **Practice page: 35**

Your child will read words with prefixes such as re– (as in redo) and suffixes such as –ing (as in walking) and understand how they change the meanings of words. • **Practice page: 36**

Your child will learn to spell words that have irregular, unexpected, or confusing spellings. For example, words like would and wood sound alike but have different spellings. In words like bird, the letter r changes the vowel sound. • **Practice pages: 37, 38**

Common Core State Standards for English Language Arts*

W.2 Writing Standards

Text Types and Purposes
(Standards: W.2.1, W.2.2, W.2.3)

Your child will state an opinion in writing, giving reasons to support the opinion.
• **Practice pages: 39, 40**

Your child will write to provide facts and information about a topic. • **Practice pages: 41–44**

Your child will write stories that describe actions, thoughts, and feelings. Your child's stories should use time-order words such as first, then, and later. • **Practice pages: 45–47**

Production and Distribution of Writing
(Standards: W.2.5, W.2.6)

Your child will revise and edit writing to make sure it is correct, to make it more interesting, and to answer questions from readers. • **Practice pages: 48, 49**

Your child will write on a computer and print out his or her work to share with others.
• **Practice page: 49**

Research to Build and Present Knowledge
(Standards: W.2.7, W.2.8)

Your child will gather ideas for writing by researching and by thinking about his or her own experiences. • **Practice pages: 41–44**

L.2 Language Standards

Conventions of Standard English
(Standards: L.2.1a, L.2.1b, L.2.1c, L.2.1d, L.2.1e, L.2.1f, L.2.2a,
L.2.2b, L.2.2c, L.2.2d, L.2.2e)

Your child will learn to use collective nouns such as team, family, class, and herd to name groups of people, animals, and things. • **Practice page: 50**

Your child will learn that some words have unexpected or irregular plurals. For example, the plural of hero is heroes (not heros). • **Practice page: 51**

Your child will learn to use reflexive pronouns that refer back to the subject of a sentence and end with –self or –selves. For example, herself *is a reflexive pronoun in this sentence: Maya looked at herself in the mirror.* • **Practice page: 52**

Your child will learn that some verbs have unexpected or irregular past tense forms. For example, the past tense of tell *is* told *(not* telled*).* • **Practice pages: 10, 11**

Your child will use adjectives such as blue, noisy, *and* soft *to describe nouns. Your child will use adverbs such as* loudly *and* quickly *to describe verbs.* • **Practice pages: 43, 44, 62**

Your child will rearrange and rewrite sentences to make them shorter, longer, more detailed, or more precise. • **Practice page: 53**

Your child will learn that proper nouns, including the names of specific places, holidays, and products, should always be capitalized. • **Practice page: 54**

Your child will learn to use a comma at the end of greetings (example: Dear Grandma,) and closings (example: Your friend,). • **Practice page: 55**

Your child will learn to use apostrophes when writing possessives like Matt's *and contractions like* can't. • **Practice page: 56**

Your child will learn that certain letter combinations appear in many words. For example, the words baby, lady, *and* lazy *all end with the long e sound spelled y.* • **Practice page: 57**

Your child will learn to use a dictionary to find correct spellings of words. • **Practice page: 58**

Vocabulary Acquisition and Use
(Standards: L.2.4a, L.2.4d, L.2.4e, L.2.5a, L.2.5b)

Your child will work with compound words such as bedtime *and realize that if you know the meanings of* bed *and* time, *you know the meaning of* bedtime. • **Practice page: 60**

Your child will learn the meanings of new words by using context clues or by looking them up in a dictionary. • **Practice pages: 59, 61**

Your child will think about word meanings and how they relate to familiar experiences. He or she will distinguish between words that have very similar meanings, such as sip, drink, *and* gulp.• **Practice pages: 62, 63**

Understanding Details

Read the story.

The Ants and the Cookie

One day, two ants went exploring. They came across two giant cookies.
"These cookies are huge!" said the first ant.

"One of these cookies would feed my whole family for a month," said the
second ant. "But, how can little ants like us carry such big cookies like these?"

"It seems impossible!" said the first ant. "But, I must try."

So, the first ant started to tug and pull at one cookie. Suddenly, a tiny piece
broke off.

"I am going to take this piece back to my family," said the first ant.

"You go ahead," said the second ant. "I'm not going to waste my time on such a
small piece of cookie. I will find a way to take the whole cookie back to my family."

So, the first ant went home with her small piece of cookie. Soon, the first ant
returned. She found the second ant still pushing and shoving the other cookie, but
he was unable to move it. Again, the first ant broke off a small piece of cookie and
took it back home. This went on for most of the day. The first ant kept carrying
small pieces of cookie back to her family until she had moved the entire cookie.
The second ant finally tired of trying to complete a task that seemed too big to do.
She went home with nothing.

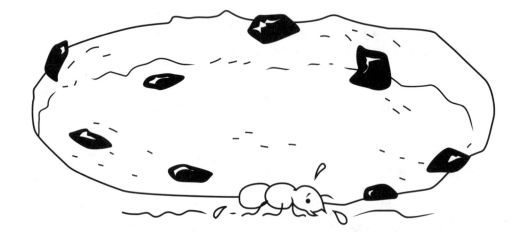

Understanding Details

Answer the questions.

1. How did the first ant carry the cookie home?
   A. She dragged it.
   B. She carried a little bit at a time.
   C. She ate most of it first.

2. What happened to the second ant?
   A. She got tired of trying and quit.
   B. She carried the cookie home.
   C. She ate the cookie.

Write the past tense of each verb (action word).

3. come _____

4. say _____

5. feed _____

6. take _____

7. go _____

8. break _____

9. keep _____

10. bite _____

Helping at Home

When your child tells you a story, put on your reporter's hat and interview your child, asking questions that begin with *who*, *what*, *where*, *when*, *why*, and *how*. Invite your child to ask questions about your stories, too.

Finding the Central Message

Read the story. Identify the lesson, or moral, of the story. Then, read each description. Decide if it describes the City Mouse, the Country Mouse, or both mice. Write an X in the correct box.

City Mouse, Country Mouse

Once upon a time, a city mouse went to visit her friend in the country. The country mouse had spent the day gathering grain and dried pieces of corn to greet her friend with a nice meal. The city mouse was surprised to find her poor friend living in a cold tree stump and eating such scraps. So, she invited the country mouse to visit her in the city. The country mouse agreed.

The country mouse could not believe her eyes when she arrived! Her friend lived in a warm hole behind the fireplace of a large home. She was even surprised to find all of the fine foods that were left behind after a party the night before. The country mouse wished that she could live in the city as well.

Suddenly, the family's cat ran in and chased the two mice away. He nearly caught the country mouse with his sharp claws. As the friends raced back to the mouse hole, the country mouse said, "I'm sorry, friend, but I would rather live a simple life eating grain and corn than live a fancy life in fear!" The country mouse went back home.

1. What is the moral of the story? _____

_____

_____

Description	City Mouse	Country Mouse
She feasted daily on fine foods.		
She would rather have a simple, safe life.		
She gathered grain and corn.		
She lived in a large house.		
She was surprised by all of the fine foods.		
She lived in a warm place.		

Helping
at Home

When your child watches an episode of a favorite TV show, ask him or her to state the main message of the show. Prompt your child by asking him or her to think about what the main character learned during the course of the story.

Thinking About Character Responses

Characters respond to major **events** and challenges in a story. They show action and emotion when they respond to events.

Read the story. Answer each question with a complete sentence.

No Broken Friendship

Matthew and Brandon have been best friends since kindergarten. One day, when Brandon was playing at Matthew's house, Brandon jumped from the swing set and landed in a strange way. "My arm!" he shouted. One look at Brandon's arm told Matthew that it was broken.

Brandon's parents took him to the hospital where the doctor took an X-ray of his arm. The doctor put a blue cast on his arm and told Brandon that his bones would grow back in place. He also reminded Brandon not to take any risks, such as playing too roughly, during the next eight weeks.

The next day, Brandon took his X-ray to school and told the class his story. They had many questions, and Brandon answered them as best as he could. Matthew asked, "Do you want to play tic-tac-toe instead of wall ball at recess today?"

"Great idea!" Brandon answered.

1. How did Brandon respond to his mishap? _____

_____

2. How did the doctor respond? _____

_____

3. How did Matthew respond? _____

_____

Rhythmic Words

This poem has the rhythm of a swing going back and forth. Read the poem aloud to someone. Try to read it with the rhythm of a swing.

The Swing

How do you like to go up in a swing,
Up in the air so blue?
Oh, I do think it is the pleasantest thing
Ever a child could do!

Up in the air and over the wall,
Till I can see so wide,
Rivers and trees and cattle and all
Over the countryside—

Till I look down on the garden green,
Down on the roof so brown—
Up in the air I go flying again,
Up in the air and down!

Robert Louis Stevenson

Helping at Home

Look carefully at the words in the poem. Ask your child to circle rhyming words and underline words that repeat. Notice together that the poem's lines alternate between long and short. Read other poems together, observing similar patterns.

Story Events

Read the story. Answer each question with a complete sentence.

The Gift

"Happy Mother's Day," Nathan said. Nathan gave his mom a large box with a pretty bow.

"What is it?" his mother asked.

"You have to guess," Nathan said. "I'll give you a hint. It's soft and blue."

"Can I wear it?" his mother asked.

"Yes," Nathan said.

"I think I know," his mother said. She opened the box. "Thank you! It is just what I wanted," she said.

Nathan's mom took the gift out of the box. She put it on over her head. She put her arms in the sleeves. It fit just right. Nathan's mother gave him a big hug.

1. How does the story begin? _____

_____

2. How does the story end? _____

_____

3. Who said, "It is just what I wanted"? _____

_____

4. Who said, "I'll give you a hint"? _____

_____

Helping at Home

Ask your child to tell you one thing that happened in the middle of the story. Ask other questions about the story, too. Ask, "Who are the characters in this story? On what day does the story take place?"

Reading Dialogue

A **skit** is a short play. It is a dialogue between characters.

Read the skit aloud with a partner. Read the words in quotes. Perform the words in italics.

Snow Fun

Joshua: "I think I see snowflakes!"
Manuel: (*surprised*)"Really? Let me take a look."
      (*Manuel walks to the window.*)
Joshua: "Do you see them? They are really falling now!"
Manuel: "You are right. The snow makes me want to play outside!"
Joshua: (*smiles*) "I think we should get dressed and build something."
Manuel: "What should we build? A snowman?"
Joshua: "I know something better that we can build!"
Manuel: "What is it?"
Joshua: (*excited*) "Let's build a snow fort!"

Answer the questions.

1. Who prefers to build a snowman?_____

2. Who prefers to build a snow fort?_____

When you read aloud with your child, assign each character's dialogue to a different reader. Invent a unique voice to use for each character. At times, stop reading and ask your child what his or her character might think about what is happening.

Comparing Stories

People from many cultures write stories in different languages but with similar themes. Read the stories from two different cultures. Then, answer the questions.

Cinderella

Once upon a time, there was a girl named Cinderella who lived with her mean stepmother and two evil stepsisters. The three women made Cinderella do all of the chores, and she was not allowed to leave the house.

A royal ball was planned, and all of the women in the town were invited to meet the prince. Cinderella's stepmother locked her in a room so that she could not go to the ball. Cinderella's animal friends found the key and unlocked the door. But, Cinderella did not have a dress to wear. She ran outside and cried.

A fairy godmother appeared. She magically gave Cinderella a dress and glass slippers. Cinderella looked beautiful! She rode to the ball in a carriage but could only stay until midnight. When she arrived, she was able to dance with the prince. Time went by quickly, and Cinderella had to leave. At midnight, her dress turned to rags! She ran and left a glass slipper on the stairs. The prince found it and kept it.

The prince's father, the king, sent his squire to every home in the town. He needed to find the woman whose foot fit into the slipper. He came to Cinderella's house, but Cinderella's stepmother had locked her in a room. Thankfully, her animal friends helped her again. Cinderella ran downstairs to the squire and tried on the shoe. It fit, and she left to meet the prince. They lived happily ever after.

Comparing Stories

Yeh-Shen

There once was a girl named Yeh-Shen who was raised by her mean stepmother. As Yeh-Shen grew older, her stepmother made her do chores. The other daughters did not have to do any work, but Yeh-Shen did.

There was a festival in town, and Yeh-Shen wanted to go. It was a special gathering where young people had fun. Yeh-Shen's stepmother and her daughters went to the festival. They told Yeh-Shen she had to stay home. Yeh-Shen secretly went to the festival after she used magic fish bones. The bones gave her a beautiful feathered dress and golden slippers. At the festival, the king saw Yeh-Shen. As he moved toward her, Yeh-Shen had to run. Her stepmother was nearby! She left behind a golden slipper, and the king picked it up.

The king ordered his soldiers to search the kingdom for the mysterious woman with the golden slipper. Many women tried on the slipper, but no one could fit in the tiny shoe. Yeh-Shen went to the king's pavilion in the night and asked to try on the slipper. It fit perfectly. The king soon married Yeh-Shen.

1. How are Yeh-Shen and Cinderella similar? Write two complete sentences.

_____

_____

_____

2. How are Yeh-Shen and Cinderella different? Write two complete sentences.

_____

_____

_____

Story Settings

> The **setting** is the place and time in which a story takes place. As a story unfolds, the setting may change. The setting gives the reader information about where the story happens.

Read the text. Then, use the information given to draw the settings that are described.

In the fight to save his tribe's land, Chief Seattle spoke of his desire to preserve the American land. In the book *Brother Eagle, Sister Sky* by Susan Jeffers (Puffin, 2002), Chief Seattle begs us to care for Earth as we would our mothers. He also questions what will become of all people if we do not.

If people use the land wisely, Earth will always have beautiful forests, oceans, and deserts full of living plants and animals.

If our land becomes too polluted, we will lose natural beauty. Factories and electrical wires will replace the forests, oceans, and deserts.

Helping at Home

Do an online search for images of paintings by the Dutch artist Jan Steen. Choose one to study with your child. Ask, "Who are the characters in the painting? Where are they? What are they doing? What happened before? What might happen next?"

Understanding Details

Read the passage. Answer each question with a complete sentence.

Night Navigators

Many people do not realize what bats do for us. Bats are some of our best nighttime insect exterminators. More than 850 kinds of bats exist in the world. Bats can be anywhere from 1.5 inches (1.3 cm) long to more than 15 inches (38 cm) long. Although most bats eat just insects, some dine on fruit and the nectar of flowers. As the only flying mammals on Earth, bats should be recognized for their contributions to people.

Aside from controlling the insect population, bats are the main pollinators and seed spreaders for many tropical trees such as mango, guava, cashew, clove, and Brazil nut. Bats use their sonar-guided ears and mouths to enjoy a nightly dinner of millions of mosquitoes, mayflies, and moths.

1. How many different kinds of bats are in the world? _____

   _____

2. What do bats like to eat?_____

   _____

3. How long can some species of bats be?_____

   _____

4. What kinds of tropical trees depend on the bat for spreading their seeds? _____

   _____

5. What helps bats find mosquitoes, mayflies, and moths?_____

   _____

Helping at Home

Choose a topic that interests your child such as dolphins or trains. Ask him or her to write five questions about it. Then, help your child find a book or Web site about the topic and read it. How many of your child's questions were answered?

Main Ideas

Main ideas of different passages can be connected because they share things in common.

Read the passage and answer the questions.

Chemicals are everywhere. They make up the air, our homes, our food, and even our bodies. Chemicals help make things different from each other. They make apples sweet and lemons sour. They make leaves green.

When chemicals mix to form something new, it is called a reaction. As a banana ripens, it turns from green to yellow. This is from chemicals changing. When you roast a marshmallow, you are watching chemicals change in a tasty way!

1. What would be a good title for the passage?
   A. Chemicals in Our Bodies
   B. Chemicals Are Tasty
   C. Chemicals Around Us

2. What is the main idea of the first paragraph?
   A. Apples are sweet.
   B. Chemicals are everywhere.
   C. Leaves are green.

3. What is the main idea of the second paragraph?
   A. Chemicals can mix to form something new.
   B. Bananas turn from green to yellow.
   C. Chocolate milk is tasty.

Helping at Home

Discuss the article and decide with your child what else you want to learn about chemicals in living things or in the air, soil, etc. Do some research and write a third paragraph. What is the new paragraph's main idea? Does it fit with the first two?

Connecting Ideas

Main ideas of different passages can be connected because they share things in common.

Read each passage. Circle the letter of the answer that tells the main idea. Then, identify the connection between the passages.

1. George Washington grew up in Virginia. He liked to play games outside. He also helped his family on their farm. When he was seven, he started school.

   A. George Washington was the first president.
   B. George Washington grew up in Virginia.
   C. George Washington went to school.

2. Abraham Lincoln had many different jobs. He worked as a farmer and a carpenter. He also helped on riverboats. He worked in a store. Later, he became a lawyer.

   A. Abraham Lincoln was born in a log cabin.
   B. Abraham Lincoln liked to read books.
   C. Abraham Lincoln had many different jobs.

3. Martin Luther King, Jr., won the Nobel Peace Prize. This prize is given to a person who has worked hard for peace. The prize is money. Martin gave the money to people who helped him work for peace.

   A. Martin Luther King, Jr., won the Nobel Peace Prize.
   B. Martin Luther King, Jr., believed all people were born equal.
   C. We celebrate Martin Luther King Day in January.

4. What do all of the passages have in common? Write a complete sentence.

   _____

   _____

Play a board game with your child, asking him or her to read the directions aloud to begin. During play, stop occasionally and ask your child to reread in order to clarify the rules. Ask, "Why is that rule important for the game?"

Words in Text

Read the passage. Focus on the bold words and think about their meanings. Underline important information.

The Koala

Koalas live in Australia. They spend most of their time high up in tall **eucalyptus** trees. Koalas eat the leaves from the trees. They eat about 2 to 3 pounds (0.9 to 1.4 kg) of leaves every day. Koalas drink very little water. The eucalyptus leaves give koalas the water they need.

Many people think koalas are bears because they look like bear cubs. Koalas are not bears. They are **marsupials**. Marsupials are a special kind of mammal. They have pouches to keep their babies warm and safe.

Koalas have pouches just like another animal whose name begins with the letter K. Can you guess what the animal is? It is a kangaroo.

Words in Text

Use the passage on page 23 to answer the questions.

1. What is the passage about?
    A. Australia
    B. koalas
    C. eucalyptus trees

2. Where do koalas spend most of their time?
    A. in eucalyptus trees
    B. in their mothers' pouches
    C. in caves with bears

3. What is a *marsupial*?
    A. a mammal with a pouch
    B. an animal that swims underwater
    C. a mammal with a long trunk

4. What is *eucalyptus*?
    A. a type of marsupial
    B. a type of tree
    C. a baby koala

Write the plural of each word.

5. koala   _____

6. marsupial   _____

7. pouch   _____

8. baby   _____

9. leaf   _____

Helping at Home

Let your child decorate a craft stick with question marks and a pair of eyes. When reading together, let your child point the stick at unknown words. Then, search the surrounding words for clues to the new word's meaning.

Using Graphics

Charts and tables are helpful for organizing information. To read a chart, match the given information from the top and the side to find new information in the boxes.

Use the chart to answer the questions.

	Monday	Tuesday	Wednesday	Thursday	Friday
Reading	Unit 1	Unit 2	Unit 3	Unit 4	Unit 5
Writing	brainstorming ideas	rough draft	revised writing	edited writing	final draft
Math	pp. 21–22	pp. 23–24	pp. 25–26	pp. 27–30	line graph
Science	plant seeds		recording sheet		recording sheet
Social Studies		map		time line	

1. What assignment is due on Wednesday in science? _____

2. What assignment is due on Thursday in writing? _____

3. On what day is the time line due in social studies? _____

4. In what subject do we read pages 23–24 on Tuesday? _____

5. What assignment is due on Monday in social studies? _____

6. On what day is Unit 3 due in reading? _____

7. On what day is the line graph due in math? _____

8. What assignment is due Tuesday in writing? _____

Helping at Home

Have your child research the current school lunch menu and write or type the information in the form of a chart. Suggest that your child use lines, colors, illustrations, or other features to make the information clear and well-organized.

Using Graphics

Use the schedule to answer the questions.

		Times							
		7:00	**7:30**	**8:00**	**8:30**	**9:00**	**9:30**	**10:00**	**10:30**
Channels	**2**	Quiz Game Show	Jump Start		Summer the Dog			News	
	4	Lucky Guess	You Should Know	Wednesday Night at the Movies *Friends Forever*				News	
	5	Best Friends	Mary's Secret	Where They Are	Time to Hope	Tom's Talk Show		News	
	7	123 Oak Street	Lost Alone	One More Time	Sports			News	
	11	Your Health	Eating Right	Food News		Cooking with Kate		Home Décor	Shop Now
	24	Silly Rabbit	Clyde the Clown	Balls o' Fun	Slime and Rhyme	Cartoon Alley		Fun Times	Make Me Laugh

1. What does the schedule show?
   A. times and channels of TV shows
   B. times and channels of radio shows
   C. the number of people who like different shows

2. On what channels can you watch news at 10:00?
   A. 2, 5, and 11
   B. 3, 4, and 11
   C. 2, 4, 5, and 7

3. What time is the show "Silly Rabbit" on?
   A. 7:00
   B. 7:30
   C. 8:30

Helping at Home

Look through a print or online newspaper with your child. Notice what information is given in paragraphs and what facts are presented in charts, graphs, maps, or other formats. Talk about how to read graphics and why they are useful.

Author's Purpose

Read the passage and answer the questions.

Cars Then and Now

Have you ever been in a convertible car? If you had lived long ago when Henry Ford started making cars, you may have owned a convertible. Henry Ford built all kinds of cars. He built the first cars that were low enough in price for many people to buy them. The cars could not go as fast as the cars today, but they looked like a lot of fun!

Henry Ford's cars were different from the cars that you see today. The cars used gas, but the tanks were under the drivers' seats. People had to lift the seats to put gas in the cars. Sometimes, the cars would not start in the cold weather unless people poured hot water under the hoods. Many of the cars did not have bumpers or mirrors because those things cost extra money. Still, they were a great way to get around, just as our cars are today.

1. What is the author's purpose? _____

_____

2. Would you rather have a car from the past or a car from today? Make a list of similarities and differences to help you decide.

How Cars of the Past and Cars of Today Are Similar

A. _____

B. _____

How Cars of the Past and Cars of Today Are Different

A. _____

B. _____

Helping at Home

When visiting the library, ask your child to find five fiction or nonfiction books about dogs, outer space, or another topic. Skim each book and ask your child to think about why the author wrote it. To inform? To entertain? To persuade?

Finding Reasons

Read the passage. Answer each question with a complete sentence.

Germs

Germs are things we do not want to share. Germs can make people sick. Even though we cannot see germs, they get into the body in many ways. Germs can get into the body through the nose, mouth, eyes, and cuts in the skin. We share germs when we drink from the same cups or eat off of the same plates.

Here are some helpful tips to keep germs to yourself and to stay healthy:

- Wash your hands with soap.
- Cover your mouth when you cough or sneeze.
- Do not share food or drinks.
- Keep your fingers out of your nose and mouth.
- Do not rub your eyes.
- Get a little bit of sunshine and fresh air.
- Eat healthful meals.
- Get plenty of sleep.

1. Why does the author suggest to keep germs to yourself? _____

_____

2. Why should you cover your mouth when you sneeze or cough? _____

_____

Helping at Home

Ask your child to design a poster explaining why family members should brush their teeth, eat fruits and vegetables, exercise, or practice another healthy habit. It should include at least three good reasons. Display the poster in your home.

Comparing Texts

Read each text about safety. Think about how they are the same and different.

Wearing a helmet is important when riding a bike. Boys and girls ride bikes on grass and on sidewalks. The different types of ground can be tricky when riding. Animal holes are hidden in the grass. Rocks and sand are on sidewalks. By wearing helmets, boys and girls keep their heads safe.

Gardening gloves are useful. They protect our hands and wrists from pesky prickles. Rose bushes can have many sharp thorns. Gloves also keep hands safe from sunburn while outdoors in a sunny garden. The gloves even keep hands clean. Gardens are full of moist soil. The dirt can get under nails and in between fingers. Gardening gloves are very handy!

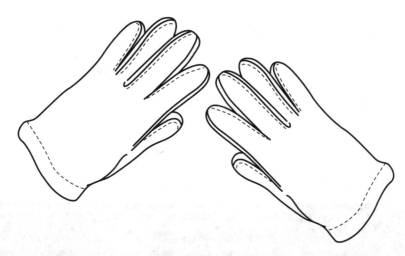

Comparing Texts

Use the texts on page 29 to answer the questions. Write in complete sentences.

1. Why is it safe to wear a helmet when riding a bike? _____

   _____

2. Why is it safe to wear gloves when gardening? _____

   _____

3. How are the two texts alike?_____

   _____

4. How are the two texts different? _____

   _____

Draw lines to connect the **verbs**, or action words, with the related verbs.

5. toss   grab

6. clutch   close

7. slam   throw

Draw lines to connect the **adjectives**, or describing words, with the related adjectives.

8. thin   tiny

9. small   gigantic

10. large   slender

Helping at Home

After a fun outing, write three sentences explaining what you enjoyed most and invite your child to do the same. Then, compare the two texts. What is similar? What is different? What adjectives and verbs can your child find in the sentences?

Short Vowel Sounds

There are five main vowels: *a, e, i, o,* and *u.* The **short vowel sounds** are *a* as in *cat, e* as in *bed, i* as in *ship, o* as in *box,* and *u* as in *tub.*

Complete each word with the correct short vowel sound.

 1. c ____ p

 2. d ____ t

 3. l ____ g

 4. f ____ n

 5. m ____ p

 6. l ____ ps

 7. p ____ g

 8. n ____ t

 9. h ____ t

 10. tr ____ ck

Use the letters to write three short vowel words.

| l | t | b | p | n | s | i | o | u |

© Carson-Dellosa • CD-734045

Helping at Home

Say words with short vowels, such as *bat, hot, set, lid,* and *run.* For each, have your child show the vowel letter with his or her hands: *A* (tipi shape), *E* (three fingers out), *I* (one finger out), *O* (circle shape) or *U* (curved up).

Long Vowel Sounds

When a letter sounds like its name, it makes a **long vowel sound**.

Examples: *a* as in *t*<u>*a*</u>*ke*, *i* as in *l*<u>*i*</u>*ke*

When a word has a consonant-vowel-consonant-e pattern (CVCe), the vowel sound is usually long, and the *e* is silent.

Examples: *name, ride, note, cute*

Complete each word with the correct long vowel sound and a silent *e*.

 1. c ____ p ____

 2. c ____ k ____

 3. br ____ d ____

 4. airpl ____ n ____

 5. b ____ n ____

 6. k ____ t ____

 7. r ____ k ____

 8. p ____ p ____

 9. m ____ l ____

 10. c ____ n ____

 11. c ____ n ____

 12. t ____ p ____

 Helping at Home Write *e* on a special sticker or on a star shape cut from paper. Have your child write three-letter words such as *cap, fin,* and *cut,* then add the super silent *e* to the end to make new words with long vowel sounds.

Vowel Teams

Vowel digraphs are two vowels next to each other that usually make one sound. The vowel digraphs *ai, ea, ee,* and *oa* often make a long vowel sound.

Examples: *w<u>ai</u>t, r<u>ea</u>l, b<u>ee</u>, g<u>oa</u>t*

Read each clue. Complete each word with the correct vowel digraph.

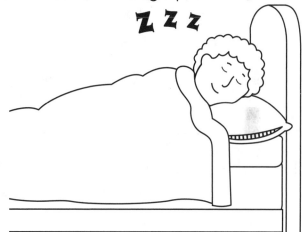

1. You do this when you are tired.

   sl _____ _____ p

2. This is water that falls from the sky.

   r _____ _____ n

3. You use this in the bath.

   s _____ _____ p

4. Jack carried this up a hill.

   p _____ _____ l

5. You ride in this on the water.

   b _____ _____ t

6. You play in the sand there.

   b _____ _____ ch

7. You do this with your eyes.

   s _____ _____

Helping at Home

Draw a pennant shape on a card and write these vowel teams inside: *ai, ea, ee, oa.* Keep the card handy when you read with your child. Can your child find any words with the vowel teams? If so, say the words, stretching out the long vowel sound.

Vowel Teams

These letter combinations also make special sounds.

ou *mouse*	ow *flower*	oi *coin*	oy *boy*	ew *news*

Use the words from the word bank to label the pictures.

boil	chew	cloud	crown	growl	house
jewel	mouth	point	screw	soil	tower

1.	2.	3.
_____	_____	_____
4.	5.	6.
_____	_____	_____
7.	8.	9.
_____	_____	_____
10.	11.	12.
_____	_____	_____

Helping at Home

Ask your child to draw vowel teams such as *oi* or *ou* as cartoon characters who are dressed alike and holding hands. What letters can be added before and after the vowel teams to make words?

Syllables and Vowel Sounds

All words have parts called **syllables**. The number of syllables in a word is the same as the number of vowel sounds you hear in the word.

Examples: *nine* = one syllable and one vowel sound
zebra = two syllables and two vowel sounds

Complete the table.

Words	Syllables	Vowel Sounds	Words	Syllables	Vowel Sounds
1. apron	2	2	6. playful		
2. three			7. lady		
3. nail			8. favorite		
4. window			9. grape		
5. relaxing			10. sweet		

Sort the words above by the number of syllables.

1	2	3

Prefixes and Suffixes

A **prefix** is a part of a word. It is at the beginning of many words. It is a syllable. Add one prefix from the word bank to each word below. Write a definition for the new word.

ex- (out)	re- (again)	sub- (under)	un- (not)

1. _____marine: _____

2. _____it: _____

3. _____do: _____

4. _____view: _____

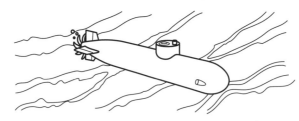

A **suffix** is a part of a word. It is at the end of many words. It can be a syllable. Add one suffix from the word bank to each word below. Write a definition for the new word.

-er (one who)	-en (made of)	-ful (full of)	-less (without)

5. play_____: _____

6. hope_____: _____

7. work_____: _____

8. wood_____: _____

Homophones

Homophones are two words that sound alike but are spelled differently and have different meanings.

Example: *tail, tale*

Write the correct homophone to complete each sentence.

1. I cannot believe you ate that _____ cake by yourself!
   (whole, hole)

2. Did you get a letter in the _____ today?
   (male, mail)

3. The _____ lives in a beautiful castle.
   (prints, prince)

4. _____ you help me with my homework?
   (Would, Wood)

5. My grandmother has a lovely _____ garden.
   (rose, rows)

6. I put my bike in the garage when it _____.
   (reigns, rains)

7. That tiger has large _____!
   (paws, pause)

8. You need two cups of _____ to make the cake.
   (flower, flour)

9. Comb your _____ before you go to school.
   (hare, hair)

10. That skunk has a strong _____!
    (cent, scent)

Check your local library for *Dear Deer* by Gene Barretta or *The King Who Rained* by Fred Gwynne. These fun and silly books are all about mixed-up homophones.

Helping at Home

R-Controlled Vowels

When *r* follows most vowels, it takes control, and the vowel makes a new sound.

Examples: *far*, *her*, *sir*, *fur*

Write the word from the word bank that best completes each sentence.

after	bird	car	dark	first	fur	stars

1. We ride in the _____ to the zoo.

2. I want to be _____ in line.

3. We see many animals with _____ .

4. The _____ has colorful feathers.

5. We will eat _____ the sea lion show.

6. It is _____ when we drive home.

7. I see many _____ in the sky.

Talk about how a vowel letter plus *r* makes a growl-like "rrrr" sound in words. Have fun with your child saying words from this page and other words with r, growling loudly for the vowel sound in each word.

Facts and Opinions

A **fact** is something you know is true. An **opinion** is what you believe about something.

Read the passage. Then, write facts and opinions from the passage.

American Indian Dances

American Indians have long used dancing to express themselves. Each dance has a deep and emotional meaning to a given tribe. The Great Plains Indian dancers dress in feathers and painted masks for the fast and colorful Fancy Dance. It is the most exciting of the dances. Other Indian dancers perform the Hoop Dance with large hoops that they swing and shape to resemble patterns from nature. It is by far the most difficult dance. The Pueblo Indian dancers, wearing butterfly headdresses, imitate the peaceful life of the butterfly with the Butterfly Dance. The dance is graceful and beautiful.

Write three facts from the passage.

1. _____

2. _____

3. _____

Write three opinions from the passage.

4. _____

5. _____

6. _____

Write one opinion of your own about the passage.

7. _____

_____

Ask your child to write several sentences describing the perfect school lunch. Remind your child to include opinion statements about why he or she thinks the foods described are the best. Do you agree or disagree with the opinions?

Facts and Opinions

Use your answers on page 39 to answer the questions.

1. Write an opinion you had after reading the passage. _____

_____

2. Why do you have this opinion? Write two sentences. Include a reason and a
   linking word from the word bank in each sentence.

also	and	because	but	or

_____

_____

_____

_____

3. Write a paragraph using this information. Include your opinion, two reasons, and a
   concluding sentence.

_____

_____

_____

_____

_____

Helping at Home
Have your child write a short review of a book or movie you own.
It should include opinions, supporting reasons, and a concluding
statement. Encourage your child to type the review, print it out, and
store it with the book or movie.

Writing a Biography

You are going to research a famous person in sports. To prepare, read about Michael Jordan in the **biography** below. A biography is a written history of a person's life. Then, answer the questions.

Michael Jordan was born on February 17, 1963, in Brooklyn, New York. He grew up in North Carolina and attended school there. His father built a basketball court in the backyard of their house. Michael and his four brothers and sisters played there.

When Michael was in high school, he played baseball. He did not make the basketball team and was very disappointed. He kept practicing basketball. By the next year, he had grown four inches! He finally made the team and went on to play in college.

Michael played so well in college that he was a professional basketball player and later an Olympic basketball player. He played for the Chicago Bulls from 1984 until 1993. Then, he decided to play baseball but soon returned to the Chicago Bulls in 1995. He is known as one of the greatest basketball players of all time.

1. What is the main idea of the biography?
   A. Michael was one of the highest-paid basketball players.
   B. Michael is one of the greatest basketball players of all time.
   C. Michael played for the Chicago Bulls.

2. What is Michael best known for?
   A. playing baseball
   B. playing basketball
   C. being born in Brooklyn, New York

3. Write *T* for each sentence that is true. Write *F* for each sentence that is false.

   _____ Michael was born in Chicago.

   _____ Michael played for the Chicago Bulls.

   _____ Michael lived in North Carolina while growing up.

Helping at Home

At the library, help your child find the biography section in the children's area. Browse the titles and help your child select several to read. Explain that these books are nonfiction because the stories they tell are true.

Writing a Biography

1. Write the name of a sport you enjoy. _____

2. Research a person who plays this sport. He or she may be a professional athlete or just a friend. If you choose a professional athlete, look for information about his or her life in books, magazines, newspapers, or on the Internet. You may do research in a library, the classroom, or at home. If you choose a friend or a person you know, ask about his or her life in person or on the phone.

3. Gather information about the person's life. Complete the research organizer below.

Name of athlete	
Date of birth	
Place of birth	
Childhood information	
Sport played	
Team name	
Known for (famous fact)	

4. Why does he or she play the sport? Write a complete sentence.

_____

_____

5. Write a fact you learned.

_____

_____

Encourage your child to continue the project on this page by writing a paragraph about the athlete. Use the passage on page 41 as a model. Encourage your child to write a clean copy or to type and print a copy and display it with a photo of the athlete.

Helping at Home

Writing to Inform

You are going to research your favorite place. To prepare, read the story.

Brianna's Favorite Place

Brianna lives in Newfoundland, Canada. Today, she is visiting her favorite place, high on a steep cliff that overlooks the ocean. She likes to watch the fishing boats bob like corks in the blue water. She listens to the sounds of the seagulls as they look for food. She admires the beauty of the tall lighthouse. She laughs as she watches the whales play. Brianna lies on her back. She clearly sees animals in the clouds. Brianna loves to feel the mist from the ocean against her face. It is a peaceful day.

All of a sudden, a huge wave swiftly crashes into the shore. The fishing boats start coming to port as fast as they can. The clouds quickly darken. A strong wind begins to blow. A foghorn cries out. It warns the sailors that a storm is coming. The waves rapidly get bigger and bigger.

As the storm comes in, Brianna is glad that she is high above the angry ocean. She takes one last look at the beautiful white-capped waves. Then, she runs home.

1. **Adverbs** are words that describe verbs. They make writing more interesting and detailed. Write the adverb from the story that describes each verb.

   A. _____ sees

   B. _____ crashes

   C. _____ darken

   D. _____ get

2. **Adjectives** are words that describe nouns. They liven up writing. Write the adjective from the story that describes each noun.

   A. _____ cliff

   B. _____ water

   C. _____ day

   D. _____ wave

   E. _____ wind

   F. _____ ocean

Helping at Home

Think of a place you and your child know and love. It could be a nearby park, a vacation spot, or a grandparent's house. Talk about how the place looks, feels, sounds, smells, and tastes. Brainstorm and write 12 adjectives that describe it.

Writing to Inform

1. Where is your favorite place?_____

2. Why is it your favorite place? Write a complete sentence. _____

_____

_____

3. Research your favorite place. Read about your favorite place in books, magazines, newspapers, or on the Internet. You may do research in a library, the classroom, or at home.

4. Gather facts from your research. Make a list of facts about your favorite place.

| My favorite place is _____. |
| Fact 1: |
| Fact 2: |
| Fact 3: |
| Fact 4: |
| Fact 5: |

© Carson-Dellosa • CD-734045

Helping at Home
Encourage your child to continue the project on this page, using the facts listed to create a travel brochure that gives facts about the favorite place. Ask your child to type the brochure, include photos or illustrations, and print it for sharing.

Writing a Story

A **brainstorm** is a group of ideas that are about one topic. Writing a brainstorm helps you recognize important details of a topic.

1. Complete the brainstorm below. The topic, *Story*, is in the circle. The lines are for your story ideas. What would you like to write about? Be creative!

Story

2. Circle the story idea you like best. Write it. _____

_____

3. Why did you choose this story idea? Write a complete sentence. _____

_____

_____

4. Write a list of characters that will appear in your story. Include at least two characters.

_____

_____

Helping at Home Help your child brainstorm ideas for personal narratives (stories about your child's real experiences), realistic fiction stories (made-up stories about ordinary characters and situations), and fantasy or science fiction stories.

Writing a Story

A story includes characters, setting, and plot. These are called **story elements**. Follow the steps below and use page 45 to outline, or plan, a story from your brainstorm.

1. Plan at least two characters. Write their names and three words to describe each one.

Character 1	Character 2
A. _____	A. _____
B. _____	B. _____
C. _____	C. _____
Character 3	Character 4
A. _____	A. _____
B. _____	B. _____
C. _____	C. _____

2. Where will your story take place? Write about the setting. _____

_____

3. What problem will your characters face? _____

_____

4. How will they solve the problem? _____

_____

Suggest that your child develop his or her story idea by drawing pictures of each character and setting where the story takes place. Alternately, your child may search online for appropriate photos. What story ideas do the pictures generate?

Helping at Home

Writing a Story

Use your outline on page 46 to draft your story. How will your plot unfold? Plan a beginning, a middle, and an end to your story.

Beginning

_____

_____

_____

_____

Middle

_____

_____

_____

_____

End

_____

_____

_____

_____

Encourage your child to introduce a problem in the beginning of the story, to have the characters confront the problem in the middle of the story, and to include a solution to the problem in the story's ending.

Revising

When you edit to make your writing better, you **revise** it. It is helpful to revise writing to be sure it is free of mistakes. Revising makes you a better writer. Look at page 47 and complete the first checklist below by yourself. Then, have a friend look at page 47 and complete the second checklist. This is called **peer editing**.

Revision Points	Notes—Writing I Can Fix	Checked ☑
1. I used complete sentences.		
2. I used capital letters at the beginning of sentences.		
3. I used ending punctuation.		
4. I spelled all words correctly.		
5. I wrote legibly.		
6. I have story elements.		

Revision Points	Notes—Writing That Can Be Fixed	Checked ☑
1. The writer used complete sentences.		
2. The writer used capital letters at the beginning of sentences.		
3. The writer used ending punctuation.		
4. The writer spelled all words correctly.		
5. The writer wrote legibly.		
6. The writer has story elements.		

Helping at Home

In an e-mail, write a short, funny story for your child to read. Include several places where the story does not make sense as well as several errors in spelling and punctuation. Ask your child to correct the mistakes and send the story back to you.

© Carson-Dellosa • CD-734045

Publishing

When a peer or adult revises a draft, and it has been fixed, it is ready to become a final draft, or **final copy**. A final copy can be written on paper or typed on a computer. Write your story from page 47. Make sure to consider the suggestions you and your friend made on page 48. Use the space below to write your story or type it on a computer. Make sure to include a title.

_____

_____

_____

_____

_____

_____

_____

_____

_____

_____

_____

Collective Nouns

A **collective noun** names a group of things, or members. Write the collective noun from the word bank that best completes each sentence.

army	band	crew	family	group	staff	team

1. Tony went on a _____ vacation with his aunts, uncles, and cousins.

2. The boat _____ had to wash the deck and clean the sails.

3. Luis practiced with his baseball _____ at the field.

4. The _____ of teachers were in the cafeteria having a meeting.

5. Mario's rock _____ played music at the show.

6. The students got together to make a study _____ before the test.

7. The _____ wore special green-and-brown outfits at boot camp.

© Carson-Dellosa • CD-734045

Irregular Plurals

A **plural noun** is more than one thing and usually ends in the letter *s*, as in the word *books*. An **irregular plural noun** does not end like a regular plural noun. An irregular plural noun has spelling changes at the end of the word. Use the spelling rules to complete the tables.

Nouns	Rule	Irregular Plural Nouns
wolf		
leaf		
elf	Change *f* to *ve* and add -*s*	
shelf		
scarf		

Nouns	Rule	Irregular Plural Nouns
echo		
hero		
tomato	Change *o* to *oes*	
potato		
volcano		

Helping at Home

Print matching singular and plural nouns on pairs of index cards. Include regular and irregular plurals. Assemble 20 or more cards and use them to play "Go Fish" with your child. The first player to match all his or her cards wins.

Reflexive Pronouns

Write a complete sentence with each reflexive pronoun in the word bank.

| herself | himself | itself | myself | ourselves | themselves |

1. _____

_____

2. _____

_____

3. _____

_____

4. _____

_____

5. _____

_____

6. _____

_____

Helping at Home

Name people and things such as "Aunt Julie," "Dad," "a hamster," or "all the kids in your class." For each, have your child tell you the appropriate reflexive pronoun from this page that could take the place of the noun.

Sentence Patterns

A **complete sentence** has a subject, which is usually a noun. The subject is followed by a verb. Rearrange each complete sentence. Each sentence will still have a subject and a verb, but they will be in a different order.

Example: The boy watched the movie.
The movie was watched by the boy.

1. Tasha looked for her snow boots.

_____

_____

2. Felipe climbed the large tree.

_____

_____

3. Grandma cooked steak on the grill.

_____

_____

4. Connor did his homework at the kitchen table.

_____

_____

5. The girls counted the ducks in the pond.

_____

_____

Helping at Home
Say a funny sentence such as, "The friends were tired, so they stayed up all night." How many ways can your child rearrange the words and restate the sentence? Can he or she make it longer or shorter? Say it as a question or an exclamation?

Proper Nouns

Proper nouns are nouns that need to start with capital letters. A person's name is a proper noun. Holidays, business and product names, and geographic names are also proper nouns.

Rewrite the nouns so that they are proper.

Holiday Nouns (incorrect)	Holiday Proper Nouns (correct)
groundhog day	
canada day	
new year's day	
mother's day	

Business/Product Nouns (incorrect)	Business/Product Proper Nouns (correct)
mike and henry's	
sabatino's restaurant	
danny's tea shop	
yogurt yummies	

Geographic Names (incorrect)	Geographic Proper Nouns (correct)
india	
tennessee	
japan	
atlantic	

Notice nouns on signs as you and your child ride in the car. Which are common nouns (names of generic things) and which are proper nouns (names of specific things)? Do the proper nouns begin with a capital letter?

Using Commas

Commas are used in greetings and closings of letters. A comma signals a pause. When a comma is used after a greeting, it lets the reader know the body of the letter is starting. When a comma is used after a closing, it lets the reader know the letter is ending.

Read each letter. Add a comma after the greeting and the closing of each letter.

Dear Aunt Jill

How are you doing? I can't wait to meet you! Mom said you are such a fun person to be around. Do you like crafts like I do? We should go to a pottery studio to make bowls or string some beads together to make jewelry. Maybe we could even make special bracelets for each other! I look forward to meeting you in two weeks. Stay well!

Sincerely
Beth

Dear Norris

Thank you for coming to my birthday party. I enjoyed your company. I hope you had fun swimming in the pool and eating hamburgers. The toy you gave me is one of my favorites. How did you know I like tow trucks? You are a great friend. Come over again sometime soon!

Your friend
Logan

MAIL

Helping at Home

As you read with your child, point out commas and explain that they separate and provide pauses between words. Help your child write short notes or e-mails to family members and friends, including commas in the greetings and closings.

Using Apostrophes

Read the story. Complete the chart.

The Birthday Present Mix-Up

Today is Rachel's birthday. She invited four friends to her party. Each friend brought a present. Rachel's little brother mixed up the tags on the presents. Can you use the clues to put the tags on the right presents?

- Kelly's present has flowered wrapping paper and a bow.

- Kate's present is tall and has a bow.

- Megan forgot the bow on her present.

- Lisa's present has striped wrapping paper.

Write an *X* in the correct box when you know a girl *did not* bring a present. Write an *O* when you know a girl *did* bring a present.

Kate				
Kelly				
Lisa				
Megan				

An **apostrophe** is used to show possession. Circle the word that needs an apostrophe in each sentence. Write the word correctly.

1. Rachels brother is three years old. _____

2. Kates present has a big bow. _____

3. My brothers friend spent the night. _____

4. Each presents tag was missing. _____

Spelling Patterns

Spelling patterns help us identify which letters to use when spelling words. Use the word on the top of each column to help you add similar words with the same pattern.

ca**ge**	ba**dge**	b**oi**l	t**oy**

phone	**kn**ife	fa**ce**	va**se**

gem	**j**ewel	li**ft**	cli**ff**

Helping at Home

Provide a notebook or blank sheets of paper stapled together. Encourage your child to make a spelling dictionary. Each page should include a sample word at the top and more words that fit the pattern below. Begin with the words on this page.

Using a Dictionary

A **dictionary** is a book of words and their meanings. A word you look up is called an **entry word**. Guide words are found in the top corners of each dictionary page. The word on the right is the very last word on that page. **Guide words** are helpful in guiding you to the word you need in a faster manner. You can flip through the dictionary, looking only at guide words until you find the page where your word would fit.

The entry words in the word bank are out of order. Write them in alphabetical order under the correct guide words.

lamp	loud	lane	locket	learn	lot
low	large	lion	lobster	listen	love

lamb   least

1. _____   2. _____

3. _____   4. _____

licorice   loose

5. _____   6. _____

7. _____   8. _____

lost   lucky

9. _____   10. _____

11. _____   12. _____

Provide a children's dictionary or find one at the library. Have your child open to a page and read aloud the guide words. Then, guess a word that might appear on that page. Have your child check for the word you guessed. Take turns.

Helping at Home

Context Clues

Sometimes, **context clues**, along with your own ideas, will help you make a good guess at a word's meaning. Use context clues to help you choose each bold word's meaning.

1. Most small children are **forbidden** to cross the street without an adult.
   A. allowed
   B. not allowed
   C. forced

2. Tracy buttoned her **cardigan** to keep warm at the game.
   A. sweater
   B. pajamas
   C. boots

3. The autumn morning **dew** left the playground damp.
   A. clumps of snow
   B. pieces of ice
   C. drops of water

4. Dad likes to **relax** after he takes us biking.
   A. jump
   B. rest
   C. sleep

5. Our team must be **united** if we want to win the championship.
   A. working together
   B. awake
   C. dressed up

6. I remember that type of butterfly by its **distinct** markings.
   A. yellow
   B. special
   C. dirty

7. The balloon **burst** as it brushed against the brick wall.
   A. flew higher
   B. got away
   C. popped

8. Some American Indians made their **dwellings** in rock cliffs.
   A. shoes
   B. blankets
   C. homes

Helping at Home

When you read with your child and come to an unknown word, think aloud as you use different strategies to find the meaning. Search surrounding text for clues. Talk about possible meanings that fit the story. Finally, look up the word in a dictionary.

Compound Words

A **compound word** is made by joining two or more words to make a new word with a new meaning. **Example:** *fire + works = fireworks*

Complete each sentence with a compound word from the word bank.

backward	campground	cartwheels	copperhead	grandfather
hairstylist	landmark	lighthouse	snowflakes	stepladder

1. The Washington Monument is a well-known_____ .

2. The teacher said to take one step _____.

3. My mother's dad is my _____.

4. It was dark and foggy, so the sailor was happy to see the

   _____.

5. I read in my science book that _____ snakes are venomous.

6. In the gym, they showed us how to do _____.

7. We pitched our tent at a beautiful new _____.

8. When the first _____ fall, we know that winter is on its way.

9. Mom must use a _____ to reach the top kitchen cabinets.

10. The lady has an appointment with the _____ every six weeks.

On index cards, print 24 shorter words that combine to form 12 compound words such as *sunflower* and *daybreak*. Mix up the cards and lay them facedown in a grid pattern. Use the cards to play "Memory" with your child.

Using a Dictionary

The meaning of a word you look up in a dictionary is called the **definition**. If the word has more than one meaning, the definitions are numbered.

Use the dictionary entries to answer the questions.

cream \'krEm\ *noun, plural* **creams**
the yellowish-white part of milk (Butter is made from *cream*.)

crook \'kruk\ *noun, plural* **crooks**
1. a bent part; curve (My umbrella was in the *crook* of my arm.) 2. a shepherd's staff with a hook at the top 3. a person who is not honest

cry \'krI\ *verb* **cried**, **crying**
1. to shed tears; weep (Don't make the baby *cry*.) 2. to call out loudly; shout (I heard the people near the burning building *cry* for help.)

cute \'kyüt\ *adjective* **cuter**, **cutest**
delightful or pretty (That is a very *cute* puppy.)

[1.] **dash** \dash\ *verb* **dashed**, **dashing**
1. to move fast; rush (If I am late, I *dash* to my classroom.) 2. to destroy or ruin (If I hurt my ankle, it will *dash* my hopes of running in the race.)

[2.] **dash** *noun* 1. a fast movement or sudden rush (I made a *dash* for the waiting bus.) 2. a small amount

1. Which definition best fits the word *cry* as it is used in this sentence?

    The little girl cried for her mother. Definition number _____

2. List other forms of the word *cute*. _____

3. Which part of speech is the word *cream*? _____

4. Which definition best fits the word *crook* as it is used in this sentence?

    The crook stole the diamond. Definition number _____

5. What is the definition of the word *dash* as a verb? _____

    _____

Use some of these words in sentences: *bill, pitcher, duck, light, trip, match, park.* Ask your child to look up each word in a children's dictionary. Which definition of the word fits your sentence?

Making Connections with Words

Making real-world connections with words and knowing how words are used can make your writing stronger. If you can relate to words, you can use them better in your writing. It is also important to use your five senses (sight, hearing, smell, taste, and touch) when making a connection.

Use your five senses to complete the chart.

1. Describe foods that are spicy. How do they taste?	
2. Describe sandpaper. How does it feel?	
3. Describe the aroma of perfume. How does it smell?	
4. Describe the view from the top of a mountain. What does it look like?	
5. Describe the noises of a baby banging pots and pans. How does it sound?	

Name a place, event, or experience that has special meaning for your child. It could be visiting a water park or eating a mint chocolate chip ice cream cone. Take turns shouting out related words. Include adjectives, nouns, and verbs.

Helping at Home

Shades of Meaning

Many verbs are related. They have similar definitions but are slightly different. Verbs have **shades of meaning**.
Example: *toss, throw, hurl*

Tossing is gentle, throwing is firm, and hurling is rough.

Find a partner. Take turns performing the meaning of each word.

1. whisper   speak   shout

2. stroll   walk   jog

3. peek   look   stare

4. sip   drink   gulp

5. tap   touch   poke

Many adjectives are related. They have similar definitions but are slightly different. Adjectives have **shades of meaning**.
Example: *thin, slender, skinny, scrawny*

Draw lines to connect the related adjectives.

6. big   smelly

7. chilly   hot

8. boiling   dirty

9. dusty   huge

10. stinking   freezing

When you read aloud with your child and come to a familiar verb such as *walked* or adjective such as *nice*, challenge your child to provide another word with the same or similar meaning. Does the new word change the meaning of what you read?

Common Core State Standards for Math*

The following parent-friendly explanations of second grade Common Core math standards are provided to help you understand what your child will learn in school this year. Practice pages listed will help your child master each skill.

Complete Common Core State Standards may be found here: www.corestandards.org.

2.OA Operations and Algebraic Thinking

Represent and solve problems involving addition and subtraction.
(Standard: 2.OA.A.1)

Your child will use addition and subtraction within 100 to solve word problems that involve adding to, taking from, putting together, taking apart, and comparing.
• Practice pages: 68–70, 101

Add and subtract within 20.
(Standard: 2.OA.B.2)

Your child will memorize the sums of all one-digit numbers (example: 9 + 6 = 15). He or she will practice adding and subtracting within 20 until it is effortless. • Practice pages: 71–75

Work with equal groups of objects to gain foundations for multiplication.
(Standards: 2.OA.C.3, 2.OA.C.4)

Your child will learn about odd and even numbers. • Practice pages: 76, 77

Your child will add to find the total number of objects arranged in rows and columns.
• Practice page: 78

2.NBT Number and Operations in Base Ten

Understand place value.
(Standards: 2.NBT.A.1a, 2.NBT.A.1b, 2.NBT.A.2, 2.NBT.A.3, 2.NBT.A.4)

Your child will understand that 1 hundred is the same as 10 tens. • Practice page: 79

Your child will work with the numbers 100, 200, 300, 400, 500, 600, 700, 800, and 900, understanding that these numbers are made up of 1–9 hundreds, 0 tens, and 0 ones.
• Practice page: 80

Your child will skip-count by 5s, 10s, and 100s. • **Practice pages: 81, 82**

Your child will read and write numbers up to 1000. He or she will work with numerals (such as 785), number names (such as seven hundred eighty-five), and numbers in expanded form (such as 700 + 80 + 5). • **Practice pages: 83, 84**

Your child will use what he or she knows about the hundreds place, tens place, and ones place to compare three-digit numbers and decide which is greater or less. • **Practice pages: 85, 86**

**Use place value understanding and properties of operations
to add and subtract.
(Standards: 2.NBT.B.5, 2.NBT.B.6, 2.NBT.B.7, 2.NBT.B.8, 2.NBT.B.9)**

Your child will add up to 4 two-digit numbers. • **Practice page: 90**

Your child will use what he or she knows about the hundreds place, tens place, and ones place to add and subtract within 1000. • **Practice pages: 87–89, 91, 92**

Your child will practice mentally adding 10 or 100 to a given number (example: 425 + 100 = 525) and mentally subtracting 10 or 100 from a given number (example: 162 – 10 = 152).
• **Practice pages: 93, 94**

Your child will think about addition and subtraction and explain how they work based on using hundreds, tens, and ones. • **Practice page: 95**

2.MD Measurement and Data

**Measure and estimate lengths in standard units.
(Standards: 2.MD.A.1, 2.MD.A.2, 2.MD.A.3, 2.MD.A.4)**

Your child will measure length in inches, feet, centimeters, and meters using rulers, yardsticks, meter sticks, and measuring tapes. He or she will measure two objects and determine how much longer one is than the other. • **Practice pages: 96, 97, 100, 101**

Your child will measure the length of an object using different units (for example, in inches and in centimeters) and compare the two measurements. • **Practice page: 97**

Your child will estimate lengths in inches, feet, centimeters, and meters.
• **Practice pages: 98, 99**

Common Core State Standards for Math*

Relate addition and subtraction to length.
(Standards: 2.MD.B.5, 2.MD.B.6)

Your child will use addition and subtraction to solve word problems about length.
• **Practice pages: 101, 102**

Your child will work with number lines, using them to show where numbers lie on the line and to solve problems. • **Practice pages: 103, 104**

Work with time and money.
(Standards: 2.MD.C.7, 2.MD.C.8)

Your child will tell and write time to the nearest five minutes using both digital and analog clocks. • **Practice pages: 105–107**

Your child will solve word problems involving dollar bills, quarters, dimes, nickels, and pennies. • **Practice pages: 108, 109**

Represent and interpret data.
(Standards: 2.MD.D.9, 2.MD.D.10)

Your child will measure the lengths of several objects and show the data on a line plot.
• **Practice page: 110**

Your child will work with picture graphs and bar graphs to show simple data sets and answer questions about them. • **Practice pages: 111, 112**

© Carson-Dellosa • CD-734045

2.G Geometry

Reason with shapes and their attributes.
(Standards: 2.G.A.1, 2.G.A.2, 2.G.A.3)

Your child will identify triangles, quadrilaterals (four-sided shapes), pentagons, hexagons, and cubes. He or she will count their sides, angles, faces, etc. • **Practice pages: 113–115**

Your child will explore the concept of area by dividing rectangles into rows and columns of same-size squares and counting them to find the total number. • **Practice pages: 116, 117**

Your child will explore the concept of fractions by dividing shapes into two, three, or four equal sections and describing the parts as halves, thirds, and fourths. • **Practice pages: 118–121**

Word Problems

Solve each problem. You can draw pictures to help you. Show your work in the box.

1. Matt caught 4 worms. Jack caught 5 worms. Lamar caught 9 worms. How many worms did the boys catch in all?

$$\begin{array}{r} 4 \\ 5 \\ +\ 9 \\ \hline 18 \end{array}$$

_____ worms

2. Kristin picked 6 ears of corn. Jill picked 2 ears of corn. Ashley picked 8 ears of corn. How many ears of corn did the girls pick in all?

_____ ears of corn

3. Kate had 3 dogs. Kenan had 6 dogs. Andre had 4 dogs. How many dogs did they have altogether?

_____ dogs

4. At 9:00, 6 people left the party. At 9:30, 3 people left. At 10:00, 5 people left. How many people left the party in all?

_____ people

5. Nina found 3 buttons. Neil found 4 buttons. Evan found 8 buttons. How many buttons did they find in all?

_____ buttons

6. Brad had 2 blue pencils. He had 3 red pencils. He had 8 yellow pencils. How many pencils did Brad have altogether?

_____ pencils

Helping at Home

Encourage your child to write word problems about situations that are meaningful to him or her. They could be about items in a collection, friends playing a game, or food needed for a party. Can you solve the word problems your child creates?

Word Problems

Solve each problem. You can draw pictures to help you. Show your work in the box.

1. Jayla's mother planted 78 tulip bulbs. She planted 19 daffodil bulbs. How many bulbs did she plant in all? _____ bulbs		2. Maria paid 39¢ for buttons. She paid 49¢ for ribbon. How much did Maria spend altogether? _____ ¢	
3. Kit had two bags of peanuts. One bag had 24 peanuts in it. The other bag had 69 peanuts. How many peanuts did Kit have in all? _____ peanuts		4. Amy had 49¢. She found 35¢. How much money did Amy have altogether? _____ ¢	
5. Mason found 19 worms yesterday. He found 14 worms this morning. How many worms did Mason find in all? _____ worms		6. Cindy sold 47 candy bars on Monday. She sold 15 candy bars on Tuesday. How many candy bars did Cindy sell in all? _____ candy bars	

Helping at Home

Choose a number from *1–100*. Can your child write a word problem with an answer that equals that number? Write a problem for a number your child chooses for you, too.

Word Problems

Solve each problem. You can draw pictures to help you. Show your work in the box.

1. The class did 36 math problems on Monday. They did 45 problems on Wednesday. How many math problems did they do in all? _____ problems	2. Kelsey did 36 math problems. He missed 7 of the problems. How many math problems did Kelsey answer correctly? _____ problems
3. Jill did 81 math problems. Then, she did 37 more problems for extra credit. How many math problems did Jill complete in all? _____ problems	4. The class has 27 students. Ms. Walker said 19 students did all of their problems correctly. How many students missed at least 1 problem? _____ students
5. Mrs. Shaw had 96 math papers to grade. She graded 32 of the papers on Tuesday. How many papers were left to grade? _____ papers	6. Each student is trying to complete 100 math problems in one week. Nassim completed 25 the first day and 27 the second day. How many problems has Nassim completed so far? _____ problems

Helping at Home

Choose several problems on this page to read carefully with your child. Ask him or her to underline key words such as *how many in all* or *how many are left* that signal whether addition or subtraction is needed to solve the problem.

Sums of One-Digit Numbers

Complete the addition chart.

+	0	1	2	3	4	5	6	7	8	9	10
0	0										
1											
2											
3											
4											
5											
6											
7											
8											
9											
10											

Helping at Home

Admire your child's completed chart. Look at the numbers together, noticing patterns. What does your child notice about the numbers in each row? What does your child notice about the numbers in each column?

Add and Subtract Within 20

Write the equations for each fact family.

1.

_____ + _____ = _____

_____ + _____ = _____

_____ − _____ = _____

_____ − _____ = _____

2.

_____ + _____ = _____

_____ + _____ = _____

_____ − _____ = _____

_____ − _____ = _____

3.

_____ + _____ = _____

_____ + _____ = _____

_____ − _____ = _____

_____ − _____ = _____

4.

_____ + _____ = _____

_____ + _____ = _____

_____ − _____ = _____

_____ − _____ = _____

5.

_____ + _____ = _____

_____ + _____ = _____

_____ − _____ = _____

_____ − _____ = _____

6.

_____ + _____ = _____

_____ + _____ = _____

_____ − _____ = _____

_____ − _____ = _____

Add and Subtract Within 20

Solve each problem.

1. 8 +4 **12**	3 +0	6 −3	2 +8	3 −2	4 −2
2. 10 −5	2 +2	6 +2	9 −8	5 −4	11 −7
3. 12 −2	6 +4	2 +1	11 −6	2 −2	9 −4
4. 7 −4	7 +0	10 −8	4 −4	3 +2	12 −9
5. 11 −8	8 +1	2 +9	6 −2	4 −1	1 +5
6. 9 −7	0 +0	1 −1	8 +2	1 +9	10 −10

When your child gets to the last several rows on the page, challenge him or her to solve all the problems in a row in two to three minutes. Check the answers together. Praise your child's correct answers or keep practicing together to gain speed.

Helping at Home

73

Subtract Within 20

Solve each problem.

1.
$$15 - 8$$
$$13 - 7$$
$$16 - 4$$
$$18 - 18$$
$$17 - 6$$
$$14 - 7$$

2.
$$14 - 0$$
$$16 - 2$$
$$15 - 15$$
$$13 - 9$$
$$18 - 5$$
$$15 - 6$$

3.
$$17 - 0$$
$$16 - 10$$
$$14 - 3$$
$$17 - 10$$
$$16 - 0$$
$$15 - 11$$

4.
$$16 - 7$$
$$13 - 2$$
$$18 - 16$$
$$14 - 5$$
$$15 - 12$$
$$17 - 11$$

5.
$$18 - 1$$
$$14 - 9$$
$$16 - 3$$
$$17 - 8$$
$$14 - 10$$
$$15 - 5$$

6.
$$15 - 13$$
$$13 - 6$$
$$18 - 7$$
$$15 - 9$$
$$18 - 12$$
$$14 - 6$$

Helping at Home

Help your child check his or her answers to the problems on the page. Then, ask your child to think about which problems were easiest to solve. Which were the most difficult? Why? Identify specific problems that are tricky for your child.

Add and Subtract Within 20

Solve each problem.

1.	2.	3.
Example:		
11 − 1 = __10__	4 + 3 = _____	12 − 12 = _____
12 − 1 = _____	6 + 1 = _____	3 − 1 = _____
3 + 1 = _____	12 − 11 = _____	11 − 0 = _____
6 + 0 = _____	5 − 0 = _____	4 + 5 = _____
10 − 4 = _____	4 + 7 = _____	10 + 1 = _____
5 + 7 = _____	0 + 10 = _____	1 + 7 = _____
4.	**5.**	**6.**
8 + 2 = _____	11 − 4 = _____	0 + 7 = _____
2 + 9 = _____	12 − 0 = _____	6 + 5 = _____
9 − 0 = _____	5 − 3 = _____	8 − 1 = _____
0 − 0 = _____	1 + 11 = _____	11 − 7 = _____
9 − 5 = _____	8 − 0 = _____	7 + 2 = _____
6 + 4 = _____	9 − 5 = _____	5 + 6 = _____
7.	**8.**	**9.**
10 − 0 = _____	11 − 2 = _____	12 − 2 = _____
7 + 5 = _____	2 + 9 = _____	3 − 0 = _____
9 − 6 = _____	7 − 2 = _____	5 + 4 = _____
12 + 0 = _____	8 + 2 = _____	10 − 6 = _____
9 − 6 = _____	7 − 5 = _____	6 + 5 = _____
3 + 4 = _____	5 + 5 = _____	11 − 6 = _____

Helping at Home

Use this page as a model to make a math tic-tac-toe game board. In each square, write several addition and subtraction problems. Then, play the game with your child. A player who solves the problems correctly can write X or O in the box.

Odd and Even Numbers

Even numbers are 2, 4, 6, 8, and so on.
Odd numbers are 1, 3, 5, 7, and so on.

Color the balloons with odd numbers red. Color the balloons with even numbers yellow.

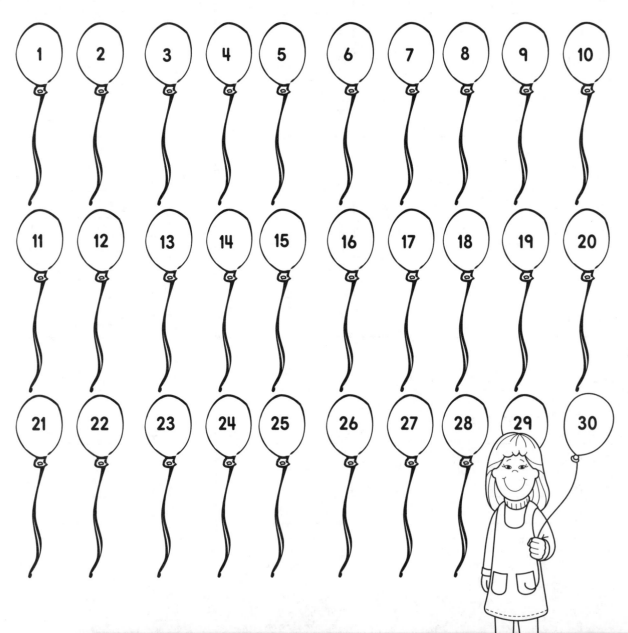

© Carson-Dellosa • CD-734045

Brainstorm with your child to think of meaningful numbers such as your child's age, your house or apartment number, your child's birthdate, or the current year. Is each number odd or even?

Helping at Home

Odd and Even Numbers

Even numbers are 2, 4, 6, 8, and so on.
Odd numbers are 1, 3, 5, 7, and so on.

Color the bubbles with odd numbers red. Color the bubbles with even numbers yellow.

Helping at Home

Play a variation of the card game "War" with your child. Divide the deck of cards and have each player lay down a card from the top of his or her pile. The player who lays down an even-numbered card wins the hand. Or, play so that the odd number wins.

Foundations for Multiplication

Count the objects in one row. Skip-count using the number of rows to find the total number of objects.

1.

There are _____ pencils.

2.

There are _____ notebooks.

3.

There are _____ erasers.

4.

There are _____ markers.

5.

There are _____ chairs.

6.

There are _____ books.

Helping at Home

Show your child how to state each item on the page as a multiplication problem. For example, for item #1, five rows of four pencils could be stated as *5 x 4 = 20*. Talk about how this is the same as skip-counting *4, 8, 12, 16, 20* to count the pencils.

Hundreds, Tens, Ones

Write how many hundreds, tens, and ones are shown. Then, write the number.

Count 1 hundred, 2 tens, and 3 ones
It is the same as the number 123.

_____**1**_____ hundred
_____**2**_____ tens
_____**3**_____ ones
= ___**123**___

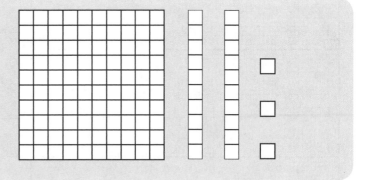

1. _____ hundred
   _____ tens
   _____ ones
   = _____

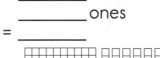

2. _____ hundred
   _____ tens
   _____ ones
   = _____

3. _____ hundreds
   _____ tens
   _____ ones
   = _____

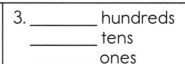

4. _____ hundreds
   _____ tens
   _____ ones
   = _____

5. _____ hundreds
   _____ tens
   _____ ones
   = _____

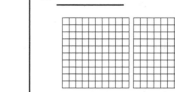

6. _____ hundreds
   _____ tens
   _____ ones
   = _____

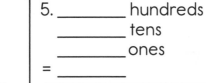

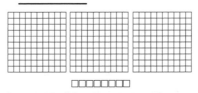

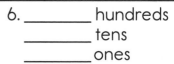

7. _____ hundreds
   _____ tens
   _____ ones
   = _____

8. _____ hundreds
   _____ tens
   _____ ones
   = _____

9. _____ hundreds
   _____ tens
   _____ ones
   = _____

Helping at Home

Play with real or pretend $1 bills, dimes, and pennies. Explain that $1 equals 100 pennies and a dime equals 10 pennies. Can your child use the money to show 126 cents? 148 cents? 112 cents?

Hundreds, Tens, Ones

Draw a line to match each number with its picture.

	100
	200
	300
	400
	500
	600
	700
	800
	900

Helping at Home

Ask your child to use a colored pencil to make vertical lines between the digits of the numbers in the right-hand column on the page (example: 6 | 0 | 0). How many hundreds are in each number? How many tens? How many ones?

Skip-Counting

Count by 5s, 10s, or 100s. Write the missing numbers on the lines.

1.   5   10   _____   20   25   _____   35   40   _____   50   55

2.   160   _____   170   175   _____   185   _____   _____   200   _____   _____

3.   300   310   _____   _____   340   350   _____   _____   380   _____   _____

4.   10   _____   _____   _____   50   _____   _____   _____   90   _____   _____

5.   450   _____   460   _____   470   _____   480   _____   490   _____   500

6.   100   200   _____   _____   500   600   _____   _____   900   1000

7.   110   115   _____   _____   130   135   _____   _____   150   _____   _____

8.   640   _____   660   _____   680   _____   700   _____   720   _____   740

9.   230   _____   240   _____   250   _____   260   _____   270   _____   280

10.   0   100   _____   300   _____   _____   600   _____   800   _____   _____

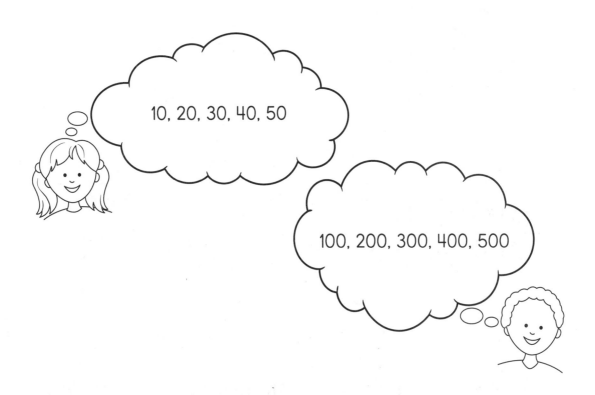

10, 20, 30, 40, 50

100, 200, 300, 400, 500

Helping at Home

Encourage your child to jump rope, skip, hop, or do another motion while skip-counting in rhythm the numbers in each row on this page.

Skip-Counting

Count the objects in one row. Skip-count using the number of rows to find the number of objects.

1. There are _____ flowers.	2. There are _____ cans.
3. There are _____ cars.	4. There are _____ magnets.
5. There are _____ coins.	6. There are _____ ducks.

Helping at Home

Gather a collection of small items such as pennies, checkers, or beads. Ask your child to arrange them in rows and columns to make them easy to count. Help your child skip-count each row to find the total number of items.

Numbers in Expanded Form

743	This number is seven hundred forty-three. Do not use the word *and* when writing or saying large numbers.

Draw a line to match each number with its number word.

1. 347 C
2. 279 G
3. 960 D
4. 719 H
5. 801 I
6. 590 J
7. 135 E
8. 509 A
9. 680 F
10. 999 B

A. five hundred nine
B. nine hundred ninety-nine
C. three hundred forty-seven
D. nine hundred sixty
E. one hundred thirty-five
F. six hundred eighty
G. two hundred seventy-nine
H. seven hundred nineteen
I. eight hundred one
J. five hundred ninety

Write the number that means the same as each number word.

11. three hundred thirteen _____313_____
12. eight hundred nine _____809_____
13. four hundred twenty-six _____426_____
14. two hundred eleven _____211_____
15. seven hundred fifty-one _____751_____
16. one hundred five _____105_____
17. five hundred thirty-two _____532_____
18. nine hundred forty-four _____944_____

Helping at Home Make several flash cards with a number on one side (example: 452) and the matching number words on the other side (example: *four hundred fifty-two*). Can your child put the numbers and number words in order from least to greatest?

Numbers in Expanded Form

Write the number that means the same.

1. 500 + 30 + 3 = _____

2. 900 + 40 + 7 = _____

3. 700 + 50 + 5 = _____

4. 400 + 70 + 9 = _____

5. 20 + 1 = _____

6. 100 + 2 = _____

7. 500 + 6 = _____

8. 90 + 8 = _____

9. 600 + 9 = _____

10. 600 + 90 + 8 = _____

Write the number in expanded form.

11. 456 _____

12. 324 _____

13. 152 _____

14. 569 _____

15. 431 _____

16. 22 _____

On nine cards or slips of paper, write *100–900*. On a second set of cards, write *10–90*. On a third set, write *1–9*. Put the cards in three stacks. Can your child draw a card from each stack and write the equivalent number?

Helping at Home

Comparing Three-Digit Numbers

The arrow points to the smaller number and opens wide to the larger number.

352 **>** 325 means 352 *is greater than* 325.

=	>	<
means *is equal to*	means *is greater than*	means *is less than*

Use >, <, or = to compare the numbers.

1. 435 〈 453

2. 712 〈 721

3. 821 〉 811

4. 741 〉 471

5. 125 〈 215

6. 345 = 345

7. 794 〈 798

8. 412 〈 421

9. 223 〈 232

10. 528 = 528

Helping at Home

Give your child a three-digit number followed by "greater" or "less than." Can your child quickly name a number that fits? Take turns giving numbers and see how quickly you can go. The first one to make a mistake is out.

Comparing Three-Digit Numbers

Use greater than (>) and less than (<) signs to compare the numbers.

1. 439 < 670

2. 944 872

3. 730 750

4. 610 603

5. 567 576

6. 887 891

7. 991 919

8. 499 500

9. 1000 998

10. 549 798

11. 473 374

12. 895 958

13. 768 391

14. 399 405

15. 818 881

16. 914 941

Helping at Home

Think aloud as you help your child solve several items on this page. Say, "First, I compare the hundreds place. If one is greater, I can stop there. Then, I compare the tens place. If one is greater, I can stop there. Finally, I compare the ones place."

Add Within 100

Solve each problem. Write the sum. Add the ones first.

1.
$$\begin{array}{r} 24 \\ +11 \\ \hline 35 \end{array}$$
$$\begin{array}{r} 16 \\ +12 \\ \hline \end{array}$$
$$\begin{array}{r} 32 \\ +21 \\ \hline \end{array}$$
$$\begin{array}{r} 16 \\ +23 \\ \hline \end{array}$$
$$\begin{array}{r} 19 \\ +20 \\ \hline \end{array}$$
$$\begin{array}{r} 24 \\ +31 \\ \hline \end{array}$$
$$\begin{array}{r} 12 \\ +43 \\ \hline \end{array}$$

2.
$$\begin{array}{r} 18 \\ +11 \\ \hline \end{array}$$
$$\begin{array}{r} 12 \\ +44 \\ \hline \end{array}$$
$$\begin{array}{r} 26 \\ +70 \\ \hline \end{array}$$
$$\begin{array}{r} 24 \\ +51 \\ \hline \end{array}$$
$$\begin{array}{r} 45 \\ +40 \\ \hline \end{array}$$
$$\begin{array}{r} 51 \\ +5 \\ \hline \end{array}$$
$$\begin{array}{r} 6 \\ +12 \\ \hline \end{array}$$

3.
$$\begin{array}{r} 17 \\ +52 \\ \hline \end{array}$$
$$\begin{array}{r} 23 \\ +43 \\ \hline \end{array}$$
$$\begin{array}{r} 73 \\ +24 \\ \hline \end{array}$$
$$\begin{array}{r} 7 \\ +12 \\ \hline \end{array}$$
$$\begin{array}{r} 25 \\ +14 \\ \hline \end{array}$$
$$\begin{array}{r} 27 \\ +20 \\ \hline \end{array}$$
$$\begin{array}{r} 30 \\ +60 \\ \hline \end{array}$$

4.
$$\begin{array}{r} 13 \\ +15 \\ \hline \end{array}$$
$$\begin{array}{r} 10 \\ +29 \\ \hline \end{array}$$
$$\begin{array}{r} 94 \\ +6 \\ \hline \end{array}$$
$$\begin{array}{r} 21 \\ +14 \\ \hline \end{array}$$
$$\begin{array}{r} 62 \\ +30 \\ \hline \end{array}$$
$$\begin{array}{r} 41 \\ +22 \\ \hline \end{array}$$
$$\begin{array}{r} 72 \\ +17 \\ \hline \end{array}$$

5.
$$\begin{array}{r} 25 \\ +10 \\ \hline \end{array}$$
$$\begin{array}{r} 22 \\ +22 \\ \hline \end{array}$$
$$\begin{array}{r} 11 \\ +24 \\ \hline \end{array}$$
$$\begin{array}{r} 4 \\ +14 \\ \hline \end{array}$$
$$\begin{array}{r} 36 \\ +11 \\ \hline \end{array}$$
$$\begin{array}{r} 12 \\ +12 \\ \hline \end{array}$$
$$\begin{array}{r} 12 \\ +13 \\ \hline \end{array}$$

6.
$$\begin{array}{r} 10 \\ +1 \\ \hline \end{array}$$
$$\begin{array}{r} 14 \\ +82 \\ \hline \end{array}$$
$$\begin{array}{r} 62 \\ +37 \\ \hline \end{array}$$
$$\begin{array}{r} 41 \\ +8 \\ \hline \end{array}$$
$$\begin{array}{r} 66 \\ +33 \\ \hline \end{array}$$
$$\begin{array}{r} 89 \\ +10 \\ \hline \end{array}$$
$$\begin{array}{r} 15 \\ +24 \\ \hline \end{array}$$

Helping at Home

Have your child use a colored pencil to draw a vertical line between the ones column and tens column in each problem. Ask him or her to circle answers less than 50 with one color and answers greater than 50 with another color.

Subtract Within 100

Subtract the ones. You cannot subtract 7 from 2, so you must regroup.	To regroup, take 1 ten from 4 tens, leaving 3 tens. Add the 1 ten to the 2 ones to make 12 ones. Then, subtract the ones: $12 - 7 = 5$.	Now, subtract the tens: $3 - 2 = 1$.
$\begin{array}{r} 42 \\ -\ 27 \\ \hline \end{array}$	$\begin{array}{r} {\scriptstyle 3\ 12} \\ 42 \\ -\ 27 \\ \hline 5 \end{array}$	$\begin{array}{r} {\scriptstyle 3\ 12} \\ 42 \\ -\ 27 \\ \hline 15 \end{array}$

Solve each problem. Remember to regroup.

1. 32 is the same as _____ tens _____ ones

2. 41 is the same as _____ tens _____ ones

3. 60 is the same as _____ tens _____ ones

4. 57 is the same as _____ tens _____ ones

5.
$\begin{array}{r} 61 \\ -\ 32 \\ \hline \end{array}$
$\begin{array}{r} 43 \\ -\ 4 \\ \hline \end{array}$
$\begin{array}{r} 20 \\ -\ 12 \\ \hline \end{array}$
$\begin{array}{r} 30 \\ -\ 16 \\ \hline \end{array}$
$\begin{array}{r} 43 \\ -\ 28 \\ \hline \end{array}$

6.
$\begin{array}{r} 80 \\ -\ 55 \\ \hline \end{array}$
$\begin{array}{r} 52 \\ -\ 17 \\ \hline \end{array}$
$\begin{array}{r} 63 \\ -\ 37 \\ \hline \end{array}$
$\begin{array}{r} 77 \\ -\ 69 \\ \hline \end{array}$
$\begin{array}{r} 66 \\ -\ 48 \\ \hline \end{array}$

Helping at Home Think aloud as you help your child solve a subtraction problem with regrouping. Explain that if there aren't enough ones to subtract in the ones column or "ones house," a ten must be borrowed from the "tens house" next door.

Subtract Within 100

Solve each problem to complete the puzzle. Regroup if necessary.

Across

B. 74 − 23 =

D. 34 − 15 =

E. 51 − 23 =

G. 52 − 28 =

I. 99 − 15 =

K. 60 − 28 =

L. 81 − 18 =

N. 54 − 33 =

P. 72 − 15 =

R. 62 − 21 =

S. 99 − 5 =

Down

A. 85 − 6 =

C. 45 − 33 =

D. 32 − 16 =

F. 98 − 12 =

H. 71 − 28 =

J. 55 − 9 =

M. 70 − 38 =

O. 37 − 23 =

Q. 84 − 5 =

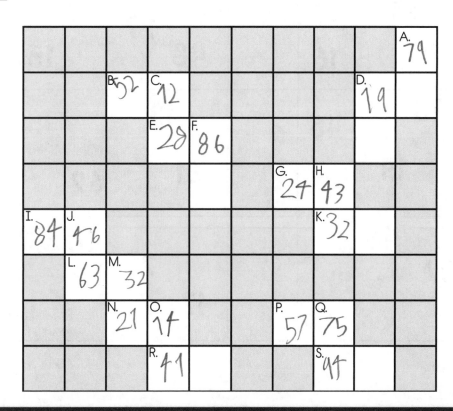

Helping at Home

Challenge your child to make a number crossword puzzle for you to solve. Ask your child if he or she plans to make the problems in your puzzle easier (with no regrouping) or harder (with regrouping).

Add Four Two-Digit Numbers

Add the four numbers in each box. Line up the numbers by the ones place. Add the ones first. Remember to write the tens you carry over the tens place, and then add.

1. 62 52 17 25	62 17 52 + 25 156	2. 13 14 41 16	
3. 60 78 38 16		4. 31 35 28 13	
5. 23 48 42 16		6. 37 27 48 15	
7. 25 45 35 19		8. 18 44 31 62	
9. 46 27 14 19		10. 46 22 17 43	

Subtract Within 1000

Solve each problem. Show your work in the box. Read the problem carefully. Then, subtract. Regroup if you need to.

1. Ryan had 427 baseball cards. He sold 109 cards. How many cards does he have left?

_____ cards

2. Kyle has 264 baseball cards. Megan has 175 cards. How many more cards does Kyle have than Megan?

_____ cards

3. Trey had 822 pennies. He took 800 pennies to the bank. How many pennies does Trey have left?

_____ pennies

4. Seth has 731 bottle caps. Brad has 947 bottle caps. How many more bottle caps does Brad have than Seth?

_____ bottle caps

5. Kade has saved $421. Her older sister has saved $540. How many more dollars does Kade's sister have than Kade?

$_____

6. Justin got $127 for his birthday. He spent $82. How much money does he have left?

$_____

Helping at Home

Show your child how to use addition to check his or her answer to each subtraction problem. Does the answer plus the bottom number in each problem equal the top number? If so, the answer is correct.

Add and Subtract Within 1000

Solve each problem. Show your work in the box. Write your answer on the line.

1. Jill picked 324 apples. Tad picked 271 apples.
   How many apples did they pick in all?

   _____ apples

2. We took a trip. On the first day, we drove 241 miles.
   On the second day, we drove 452 miles.
   How many more miles did we drive the second day
   than the first day?

   _____ miles

3. We counted 332 sunflowers in one field.
   In another field, we counted 164 sunflowers.
   How many sunflowers did we count in all?

   _____ sunflowers

4. Mrs. Lee had 567 candles for sale.
   At the end of the day, she had 325 candles left.
   How many candles did Mrs. Lee sell?

   _____ candles

5. There were 724 people at the game.
   When it began to rain, 510 people left.
   How many people stayed at the game?

   _____ people

Ask your child to look at his or her answer to each item on the page.
How close is each answer to 1000? Subtract each answer from 1000
to find out. To do this, your child may need to borrow a hundred from
the hundreds place.

Mental Math

Add by 10 or 100.

1. **+ 10**   3   13   23   ___ ___ ___ ___ ___ ___

2. **+ 10**   8   18   28   ___ ___ ___ ___ ___ ___

3. **+ 10**   26   36   ___ ___ ___ ___ ___ ___

4. **+ 10**   349   359   ___ ___ ___ ___ ___ ___

5. **+ 10**   805   ___ ___ ___ ___ ___ ___

6. **+ 100**   192   292   392   ___ ___ ___ ___ ___

7. **+ 100**   119   219   ___ ___ ___ ___ ___ ___

8. **+ 100**   188   ___ ___ ___ ___ ___ ___

9. **+ 100**   121   ___ ___ ___ ___ ___ ___

10. **+ 100**   152   ___ ___ ___ ___ ___ ___

Helping at Home

Ask your child to use a highlighter pen to highlight the digit that changes in each completed row of numbers. Ask your child, "What is the place value of this digit? Why is it easy to do the problems on this page without writing them down?"

Mental Math

Subtract by 10 or 100.

1. **– 10**   192   182   172   _____ _____ _____ _____ _____ _____

2. **– 10**   719   709   699   _____ _____ _____ _____ _____ _____

3. **– 10**   588   578   _____ _____ _____ _____ _____ _____ _____

4. **– 10**   421   411   _____ _____ _____ _____ _____ _____ _____

5. **– 10**   252   _____ _____ _____ _____ _____ _____ _____ _____

6. **– 100**   903   803   703   _____ _____ _____ _____ _____ _____

7. **– 100**   928   828   _____ _____ _____ _____ _____ _____ _____

8. **– 100**   986   886   _____ _____ _____ _____ _____ _____ _____

9. **– 100**   949   _____ _____ _____ _____ _____ _____ _____ _____

10. **– 100**   905   _____ _____ _____ _____ _____ _____ _____ _____

Ask your child to look at each row of completed answers and think of the numbers as dollar amounts. How many $10 bills would be in each amount? How many $100 bills would be in each amount?

Addition and Subtraction Strategies

Solve each problem. Show your work in the box. In the bubble below the problem, use words to explain how you solved it.

1. Sam's basketball team scored 42 points. Jay's team only scored 28 points. How many more points did Sam's team score than Jay's?

_____ points

2. Jan had 57 seashells in her collection. Her aunt sent her 26 more seashells. How many seashells does Jan have in her collection now?

_____ seashells

3. Nathan had 82 toy cars. He saved 15 special cars and gave the rest to his little cousins. How many cars did Nathan give to his cousins?

_____ cars

4. A bike shop had 43 adult bikes. They had 38 children's bikes. How many bikes did the bike shop have altogether?

_____ bikes

Helping at Home

Think aloud as you help your child solve a problem on the page. For the first item, say, "It says 'how many more,' so I know to use subtraction. I line up the ones and tens." Have your child write key words from your explanation in the thought bubble.

Measuring Length

Measure the length of each object with the ruler shown.

1. _____ inches

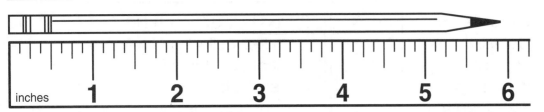

2. _____ inches

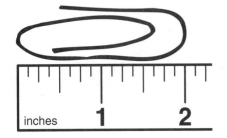

3. _____ inches

4. _____ inches

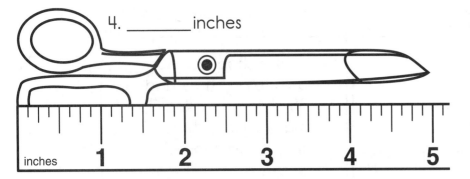

5. _____ inches

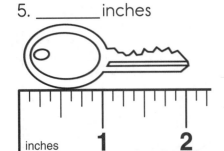

6. _____ inches

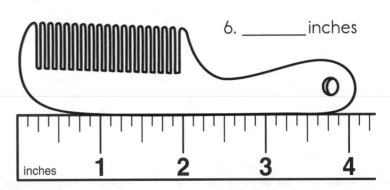

Provide a small, safe tape measure for your child to use around the house to measure lengths. Encourage your child to include the tape measure in dramatic play that takes place at imaginary construction sites, houses, office buildings, etc.

Helping at Home

Measuring Length

Measure each line with an inch ruler and then with a centimeter ruler. Write the closest number of inches (in.) and centimeters (cm) in the blanks.

1. _____ in. _____ cm

_____

2. _____ in. _____ cm

_____

3. _____ in. _____ cm

_____

4. _____ in. _____ cm

_____

5. _____ in. _____ cm

____

6. _____ in. _____ cm

_____

7. _____ in. _____ cm

_____

8. _____ in. _____ cm

_____

9. _____ in. _____ cm

_____

Helping at Home
After finding the lengths of the lines on the page, ask your child to look for things that are about those same lengths. Using a ruler will help. Prompt your child with questions like this: "Is a glove about the same length as one of the lines?"

Estimating Length

Circle the best estimate for the length of each real-life object.

1.
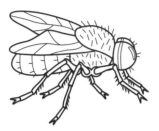
more than 10 centimeters
less than 10 centimeters

2.

more than 5 meters
less than 5 meters

3.

more than 1 meter
less than 1 meter

4.

more than 1 centimeter
less than 1 centimeter

5.

more than 2 meters
less than 2 meters

6.

more than 2 centimeters
less than 2 centimeters

Helping at Home
Point to an item in the room and guess its length. Then, have your child use a ruler to check your guess. How close did you come? Take turns guessing and verifying lengths of everyday items.

Estimating Length

Circle the best unit to measure each object.

1. The length of a car

      centimeter   meter

2. The distance from your school to the next school

      centimeter   meter

3. The length of a pencil

      centimeter   meter

4. The distance from your school to the park

      centimeter   meter

5. The distance from your house to your friend's house

      centimeter   meter

6. The length of a swimming pool

      centimeter   meter

7. The length of your pinky finger

      centimeter   meter

8. The height of a tree

      centimeter   meter

9. The width of a quarter

      centimeter   meter

Helping at Home

Help your child compare one centimeter and one meter to a unit of length on his or her body. For example, a centimeter may be about the length of your child's fingernail. A meter may be about the same as your child's height.

Comparing Lengths

Measure each line with a centimeter ruler. Write the length of the line in centimeters (cm). Use the lengths to solve the word problems.

A ────────────────── = _____ cm

B ──────────────────── = _____ cm

C ─────────────────── = _____ cm

D ───── = _____ cm

E ──────── = _____ cm

1. How much longer is line B than line A?   _____ cm

2. How much longer is line C than line D?   _____ cm

3. How much longer is line E than line D?   _____ cm

4. How much shorter is line E than line A?   _____ cm

5. How much shorter is line D than line B?   _____ cm

Helping at Home
Help your child measure and cut lengths of yarn to match the lines at the top of this page. Encourage your child to play with the yarn pieces, putting them in order from longest to shortest and using them to help answer the questions on the page.

Measurement Problems

Solve each problem. Show your work in the box.

1. Kami has 45 inches of string. She needs 13 inches to make a bracelet. How many inches of string will be left after Kami makes a bracelet?

_____ inches

2. Michael has a stick that is 15 inches long. How many inches of stick will be left after Michael cuts off 1 foot?

_____ inches

Measure the sides of each shape in centimeters. Then, find the difference between the longer sides and the shorter sides.

3.

_____ – _____ = _____ cm

4.

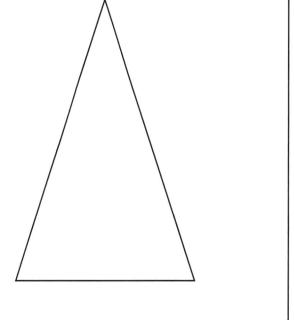

_____ – _____ = _____ cm

Helping at Home

Ask your child to look around your home for rectangular shapes such as books, tabletops, tiles, and screens. Provide a ruler so your child can measure the length of each side of the rectangles and add to find the total amount.

Measurement Problems

Solve each problem. Show your work in the box. What addition and subtraction strategies will help you solve each problem?

1. Brad's puppy is 8 inches long. His dog is 26 inches long. How much longer is his dog than his puppy? _____ inches	2. Patsy planted a sunflower that was 6 inches tall. It grew another 72 inches. How tall is the sunflower now? _____ inches
3. Carlos has a 40-inch piece of string. He cut off 15 inches. How much string is left? _____ inches	4. Neil dug a hole 25 centimeters deep. He needs the hole to be 50 centimeters deep. How many more centimeters does Neil need to dig? _____ centimeters
5. Malia cut off 3 feet of yarn. She has 5 feet of yarn left. How much yarn did Malia start with? _____ feet	6. Tia is 95 centimeters tall. Her sister is 12 centimeters shorter than Tia. How tall is Tia's sister? _____ centimeters

Ask your child to determine the height of each member of your family and record it in inches. Then, challenge your child to write word problems based on the measurements. Can you solve the problems your child wrote?

Using Number Lines

Mark has 37 goldfish. The castle has 8 fish swimming in it. The bridge has 11 fish swimming under it. How many fish are swimming in the open?

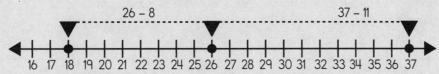

18 goldfish are not in the castle or under the bridge.

Read and solve each problem. Use the number line to show your work.

1. Nathan's dad is 32 years old. Nathan's aunt is 4 years older than his dad. How old is Nathan's aunt?

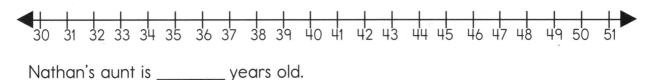

Nathan's aunt is _____ years old.

2. Beth bought 98 pencils. She gave 41 pencils away. How many pencils did Beth have left?

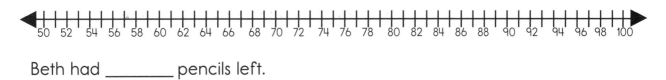

Beth had _____ pencils left.

3. The park had 14 children playing on the playground. The zoo had 29 children learning about polar bears. How many more children were at the zoo than at the park?

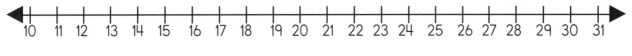

The zoo had _____ more children.

Helping at Home
Draw a large number line outside with sidewalk chalk or use masking tape to make one on the floor inside. Provide simple math problems and have your child walk or jump along the number line to find the answer.

Using Number Lines

Read and solve each problem. Use the number line to show your work.

1. Byron had 64 cars. He got 18 more for his birthday. How many cars did Byron have altogether?

Byron had _____ cars.

2. Mrs. Prasad's first grade class made 22 snowballs. Mr. Wagner's second grade class made 27 snowballs. How many more snowballs did Mr. Wagner's class make than Mrs. Prasad's?

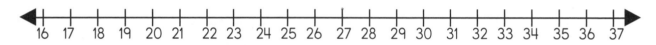

Mr. Wagner's class made _____ more snowballs.

3. Hugo had 15 books on one shelf, 14 books on a second shelf, and 16 books on a third shelf. How many books does Hugo have on the three shelves?

Hugo has _____ books on the three shelves.

4. Janelle collected fruit for the class. She collected 25 oranges, 13 apples, and 7 bananas. How many more oranges did Janelle collect than bananas and apples?

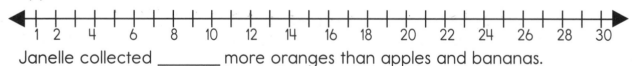

Janelle collected _____ more oranges than apples and bananas.

Position a ruler or yardstick horizontally on a tabletop and encourage your child to use it as a number line. Provide simple math problems and ask your child to "walk" his or her fingertip along the numbers to find the answer.

Telling Time

Write the time shown on each clock.

1.	2.	3.
4.	5.	6.
7.	8.	9.
10.	11.	12.

Helping at Home

When you are out with your child at stores, restaurants, and other public places, be on the lookout for analog clocks. Help your child read the positions of the hands and determine the time. Compare to times shown digitally on your phone or another device.

Telling Time

Draw the hands on each clock to show the time.

1.

6:05

2.

9:35

3.

1:15

4.

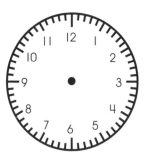

2:40

5.

11:20

6.

3:55

Telling Time

Write the time shown on each clock. Write the time two ways.

1. **8:15** or **15** minutes after **8** o'clock	2. _____ or _____ minutes after _____ o'clock
3. _____ or _____ minutes after _____ o'clock	4. _____ or _____ minutes after _____ o'clock
5. _____ or _____ minutes after _____ o'clock	6. _____ or _____ minutes after _____ o'clock
7. _____ or _____ minutes after _____ o'clock	8. _____ or _____ minutes after _____ o'clock

Helping at Home

At different times, tell your child what time it is and challenge him or her to restate that time in terms of "minutes after" or "minutes until" the hour. Ask your child to think about things that usually happen around that time of day.

Problems with Money

Solve each problem. Then, answer each question.

1. Tony has 2 quarters and 1 dime. Does he have enough money to buy a toy truck that costs 75¢? yes no Tony has _____¢.	2. Holly has 3 dimes and 4 nickels. Does she have enough to buy a toy yo-yo that costs 25¢? yes no Holly has _____¢.
3. Mom gave Denise 3 quarters and 2 dimes to buy milk. The milk costs 92¢ per quart. Does Denise have enough to buy a quart of milk? yes no Denise has _____¢.	4. Tyrone has 2 dimes, 1 nickel, and 4 pennies. Does he have enough to buy a toy train that costs 46¢? yes no Tyrone has _____¢.
5. If you had 1 half-dollar and 3 dimes, could you buy a kite that costs 95¢? yes no You have _____¢.	6. Greg has 8 nickels and 9 pennies. Does he have enough to buy a notebook that costs 50¢? yes no Greg has _____¢.
7. Jack wants to buy a toy duck. It costs 67¢. Jack has 4 quarters. Does he have enough to buy the duck? yes no Jack has _____¢.	8. Kelly has 1 quarter, 2 dimes, 2 nickels, and 3 pennies. She wants to buy a box of crayons that costs 75¢. Does she have enough? yes no Kelly has _____¢.

Helping at Home — Provide real or pretend quarters, dimes, nickels, and pennies. Encourage your child to use them to represent money amounts from each problem on the page. How many more coins would be needed to make $1.00?

Problems with Money

Mario wants to buy a game that costs $23.00. He has $17.00. How much more money does Mario need?

$23.00
−$17.00
$ 6.00

Subtract $17.00 from $23.00 to find out how much more money Mario needs. He needs $6.00.

Solve each problem. Show your work in the box.

1. Grace had $17.22. Then, she earned $5.00 for helping her mother. How much money does Grace have now?

   $ _____

2. Matt has $18.77. He wants to buy a CD for $14.50. How much money will Matt have left if he buys the CD?

   $ _____

3. Josh got $3.50 from his mother, $4.00 from his father, and $10.00 from his grandparents. How much money did Josh get altogether?

   $ _____

4. Luis has $53.00. He is trying to earn money for a bike that costs $87.00. How much more money does Luis need?

   $ _____

5. Drew earned $20.00 for mowing the yard. He already had $12.00. How much money does Drew have now?

   $ _____

6. Emma wants to buy a science kit that costs $18.00. She only has $6.00. How much more money does Emma need?

   $ _____

Helping at Home

Talk about the decimal point used on this page, explaining that it divides dollars and cents. Remind your child to set up each problem carefully, making sure that decimal points align. Each answer should include a decimal point, too.

Using a Line Plot

Place **X**s to show the toy heights on the line plot. The first one has been done for you. Then, answer the questions.

rabbit—12 inches   car—6 inches   block—4 inches

clock—8 inches   train—4 inches   football—6 inches

dollhouse—9 inches   doll—10 inches   basketball—10 inches

trampoline—12 inches   skateboard—6 inches   camera—5 inches

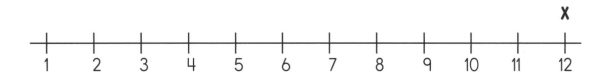

1. Which height shows up most often? _____

2. Which heights are not shown by this set of toys? _____

3. Which heights only show up once? _____

4. How many toys are 4 inches in height? _____

5. How many toys are 12 inches in height? _____

6. What is the shortest height shown by this set of toys? _____

Using a Graph

Read the graph. Then, use the graph to answer the questions.

Books We Have Read

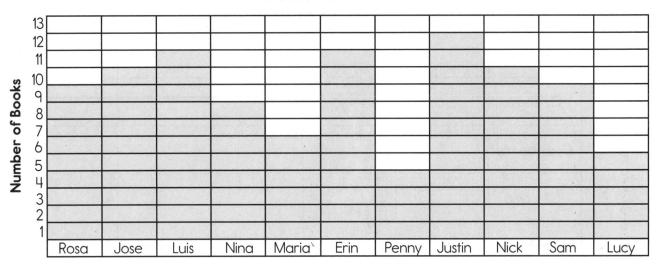

1. How many books did Erin read? _____

2. Who read more books, Luis or Nina? _____

3. Who read the most books? _____

4. Who read the fewest books? _____

5. How many books did Lucy, Sam, and Maria read altogether? _____

Helping at Home

Ask more questions about the graph on this page. For example, ask, "How would the graph change if a student were added? How would it change if a student read 17 books? What would a similar graph look like for the students in your class?"

Using a Graph

Use the data to fill in the picture graph. Draw frozen treat symbols in the boxes to show each number.

Favorite Frozen Fruit Treats at Armstrong Elementary

Type of Frozen Treat					
Grape					
Orange					
Cranberry					
Cherry					
Strawberry					
Kiwi					
Apple					

Number of Frozen Fruit Treats Eaten

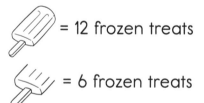

= 12 frozen treats

= 6 frozen treats

Students ate 30 grape frozen treats.

Students ate 30 orange frozen treats.

Students ate 36 cranberry frozen treats.

Students ate 48 cherry frozen treats.

Students ate 60 strawberry frozen treats.

Students ate 36 kiwi frozen treats.

Students ate 12 apple frozen treats.

Admire your child's completed graph. Think aloud as you read the information. Say, "I see that the most popular flavor of treat is strawberry. I see that grape and orange are equally popular." Encourage your child to make observations, too.

Drawing Shapes

Connect the dots to form different geometric shapes.

1. Connect the dots to form a triangle.	2. Connect the dots to form a square.
3. Connect the dots to form a trapezoid.	4. Connect the dots to form a rhombus.
5. Connect the dots to form a rectangle.	6. Connect the dots to form a hexagon.
7. Connect the dots to form a parallelogram.	8. Connect the dots to form a pentagon.

Helping at Home

Pound 25 small nails halfway into an old piece of wood to form a grid pattern. Make sure to sand the edges of the wood and secure nails tightly. Provide large rubber bands your child can wrap around the nails to make a variety of shapes.

Shapes

When three or more line segments come together, they form a **polygon**.

A polygon with 3 sides is a **triangle**.

A polygon with 4 sides is a **quadrilateral**.

A polygon with 5 sides is a **pentagon**.

Look at each polygon. Count how many sides it has. Write its name on the line.

1.	2.	3.	4.
_____	_____	_____	_____
5.	6.	7.	8.
_____	_____	_____	_____
9.	10.	11.	12.
_____	_____	_____	_____

Helping at Home

Provide craft sticks and encourage your child to use them to build shapes. How many different shapes can be made with three sticks? Four sticks? Five sticks? What is the name of each shape?

Shapes

A **quadrilateral** is any shape with four sides.

Look at each shape. Count how many sides it has. Answer the questions.

square

rectangle

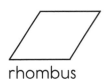
trapezoid

rhombus

circle

triangle

pentagon

hexagon

octagon

1. Name the shapes that are quadrilaterals.

_____   _____

_____   _____

2. What is the only quadrilateral with four equal sides? _____

3. What shape has three sides and three angles? _____

4. What shape has no sides? _____

5. What shape has five sides? _____

6. What shape has six sides? _____

7. What shape has eight sides? _____

8. How is a square different from a rectangle? _____

_____

Helping at Home

Talk about prefixes that have meanings related to numbers. *Tri–* means "three," *pent–* means "five," *hex–* means "six," and *oct–* means "eight." How do these relate to the names of shapes? How do they relate to words such as *tricycle* and *octopus*?

Dividing a Rectangle

Jack is planting a garden. Help him plan where to put his plants. He wants to use only a certain number of each plant. The area for each kind of plant should form a square or a rectangle. When you are finished, color the area for each plant a different color.

corn—14 plants   pumpkins—3 plants

tomatoes—10 plants   lettuce—6 plants

peppers—9 plants   squash—4 plants

beans—3 plants

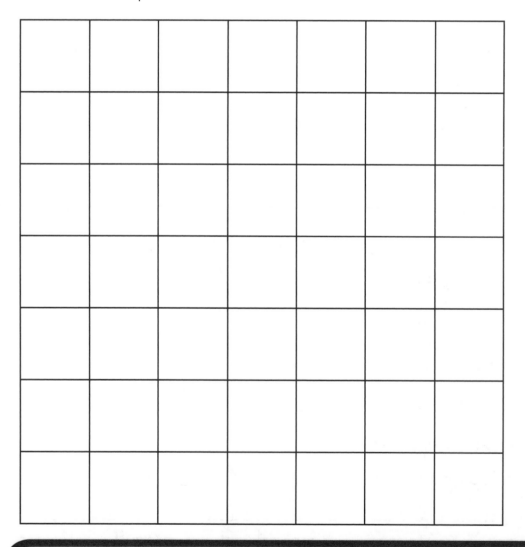

Provide graph paper with large squares or print some from a free Web site. By cutting on the lines of the graph paper, how many different squares and rectangles can your child cut out that are made up of 12 squares? 24 squares?

Dividing a Rectangle

Use the grid paper to solve each problem. Think about how squares can be used in rows and columns.

1. How many rectangles can be made from 10 squares? _____

2. How many rectangles can be made from 12 squares? _____

3. How many rectangles can be made from 15 squares? _____

4. How many rectangles can be made from 18 squares? _____

5. How many rectangles can be made from 20 squares? _____

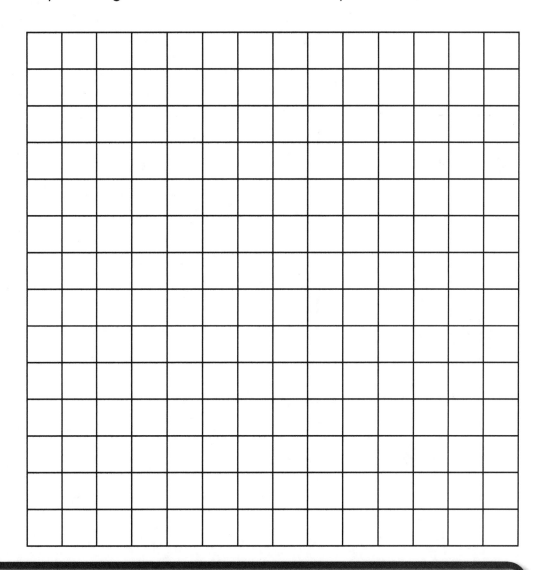

Helping at Home

Serve your child a snack of square crackers or dry cereal pieces. How many different squares and rectangles can your child compose from 6 pieces? 10 pieces? More? How are the shapes similar and different?

Understanding Fractions

A **fraction** tells parts of a whole.
The top number tells how many parts are shaded.
The bottom number tells how many parts in all.

Parts shaded ⟶ $\dfrac{1}{4}$
Parts in all ⟶

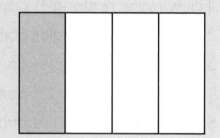

Write the number in each fraction that tells how much is shaded.

1. 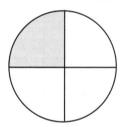 $\dfrac{}{4}$

2. 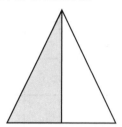 $\dfrac{}{2}$

3. 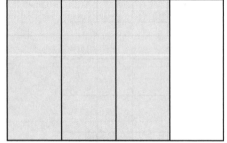 $\dfrac{}{4}$

4. 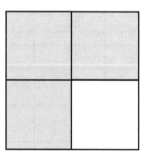 $\dfrac{}{4}$

5. 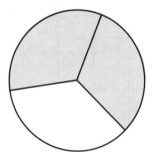 $\dfrac{}{3}$

6. 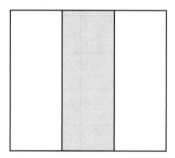 $\dfrac{}{3}$

© Carson-Dellosa • CD-734045

Helping at Home
Draw rectangles, squares, circles, and triangles on a blank page. Photocopy the sheet, cut the shapes from the copied page, and cut each shape into halves, thirds, or fourths. Let your child assemble the pieces over the whole shapes on the original page.

Understanding Fractions

Circle each fraction that tells how much is shaded.

1. 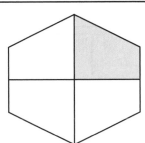 $\dfrac{1}{2}$ $\dfrac{1}{4}$ $\dfrac{1}{3}$	2. 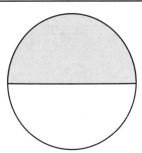 $\dfrac{1}{3}$ $\dfrac{2}{3}$ $\dfrac{1}{2}$
3. 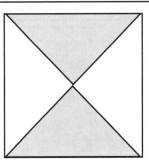 $\dfrac{2}{4}$ $\dfrac{3}{4}$ $\dfrac{1}{4}$	4. 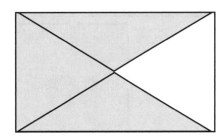 $\dfrac{1}{4}$ $\dfrac{2}{4}$ $\dfrac{3}{4}$
5. 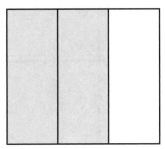 $\dfrac{1}{3}$ $\dfrac{1}{2}$ $\dfrac{2}{3}$	6. 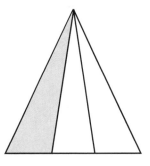 $\dfrac{1}{3}$ $\dfrac{2}{3}$ $\dfrac{1}{2}$

© Carson-Dellosa • CD-734045

Helping at Home

Draw large circles, triangles, rectangles, and squares on blank paper. Give directions to your child such as "color half of the circle green," or "make two-thirds of the rectangle polka-dotted." Have your child cut out and reassemble the divided shapes.

Understanding Fractions

Divide each rectangle into the total number of parts. Then, color the parts to show the fraction. Write the words for the fraction you colored.

1.

$\frac{1}{2}$

_____

2.

$\frac{2}{4}$

_____

3.

$\frac{1}{3}$

_____

4.

$\frac{3}{4}$

_____

5.

$\frac{1}{4}$

_____

6.

$\frac{2}{3}$

_____

Helping at Home

Provide a snack of graham crackers that can be easily snapped into fourths. Encourage your child to divide, arrange, and reassemble the crackers. Ask, "How many fourths make a whole? How many fourths make a half?"

Understanding Fractions

Divide each circle into the total number of parts. Then, color the parts to show the fraction. Write the word for the fraction you colored.

1. $\frac{1}{2}$

_____

2. $\frac{2}{4}$

_____

3. $\frac{1}{3}$

_____

4. $\frac{3}{4}$

_____

5. $\frac{1}{4}$

_____

6. $\frac{2}{3}$

_____

Answer Key

Page 11
1. B; 2. A; 3. came; 4. said;
5. fed; 6. took; 7. went; 8.
broke; 9. kept; 10. bit

Page 12
1. The moral of the story
is to be happy with what
you have. City Mouse—
first, fourth, and sixth
descriptions; Country
Mouse—second, third, and
fifth descriptions

Page 13
1. Answers will vary but
may include that Brandon
realized his arm was
broken, so he went to the
doctor. 2. Answers will
vary but may include that
the doctor put a cast on
Brandon's arm and told
him his bones would grow
back in place.
3. Answers will vary but
may include that Matthew
knew Brandon's arm was
broken, and Matthew
suggested playing tic-tac-
toe instead of wall ball
with Brandon at school.

Page 15
1. The story begins with
Nathan giving his mom
a large gift. 2. The story
ends with Mom giving
Nathan a big hug. 3. the
mother; 4. Nathan

Page 16
1. Manuel; 2. Joshua

Page 18
1. Answers will vary but
may include that both
stories have girls as the
main characters. Both girls
have slippers. 2. Answers
will vary but may include
that the two girls are
different because they
have different names.
Yeh-Shen uses magic fish
bones, and Cinderella has
a fairy godmother.

Page 19
Drawings will vary. The
first box should have
beautiful forestry, and the
second box should have a
polluted environment.

Page 20
1. more than 850; 2.
insects, fruit, nectar;
3. more than 15 inches
(38 cm) long; 4. mango,
guava, cashew, clove,
Brazil nut; 5. sonar-guided
ears and mouths

Page 21
1. C; 2. B; 3. A

Page 22
1. B; 2. C; 3. A; 4. Answers
will vary but may include
that they are all about
successful men who
helped the United
States.

Page 24
1. B; 2. A; 3. A; 4. B; 5.
koalas; 6. marsupials; 7.
pouches; 8. babies; 9.
leaves

Page 25
1. recording sheet;
2. edited writing; 3.
Thursday; 4. math; 5. No
assignment is due. 6.
Wednesday; 7. Friday; 8.
rough draft

Page 26
1. A; 2. C; 3. A

Page 27
1. The author's purpose is
to compare and contrast
old cars and new cars. 2.
Both types of cars help
people get around, are
affordable, and use gas.
Old cars had gas tanks
under the front seats. Old
cars needed hot water on
cold days. Old cars could
not go as fast as new cars
can.

Page 28
1. Answers will vary but
may include that germs
make people sick. 2.
Answers will vary but may
include that germs can
get into the bodies of
others in many ways.

Page 30
1. It protects the head.
2. They protect the hands.
3. They both deal with
safety and protection of
our bodies. 4. They deal
with safety of different
body parts (head vs.
hands). 5. toss/throw; 6.
clutch/grab; 7. slam/close;
8. thin/slender; 9. small/
tiny; 10. large/gigantic

Answer Key

Page 31

1. cup; 2. dot; 3. leg; 4. fan; 5. mop; 6. lips; 7. pig; 8. net; 9. hat; 10. truck; Words will vary but may include lip, not, bus.

Page 32

1. cape; 2. cake; 3. bride; 4. airplane; 5. bone; 6. kite; 7. rake; 8. pipe; 9. mule; 10. cone; 11. cane; 12. tape

Page 33

1. sleep; 2. rain; 3. soap; 4. pail; 5. boat; 6. beach; 7. see

Page 34

1. cloud; 2. point; 3. tower; 4. boil; 5. screw; 6. chew; 7. growl; 8. soil; 9. jewel; 10. crown; 11. mouth; 12. house

Page 35

1. 2, 2; 2. 1, 1; 3. 1, 1; 4. 2, 2; 5. 3, 3; 6. 2, 2; 7. 2, 2; 8. 3, 3; 9. 1, 1; 10. 1, 1; 1 syllable: three, nail, grape, sweet; 2 syllables: apron, window, playful, lady; 3 syllables: relaxing, favorite

Page 36

1. submarine: underwater vehicle; 2. exit: to leave; 3. undo: to take apart or redo: to do again; 4. review: to check again; 5. playful: to be full of play, lively or player: one who plays; 6. hopeless: without hope or hopeful: full of hope; 7. worker: one who works; 8. wooden: made of wood

Page 37

1. whole; 2. mail; 3. prince; 4. Would; 5. rose; 6. rains; 7. paws; 8. flour; 9. hair; 10. scent

Page 38

1. car; 2. first; 3. fur; 4. bird; 5. after; 6. dark; 7. stars

Page 39

1–3. Answers will vary but may include that American Indians use dance to express themselves. The Fancy Dance includes dancers with feathers. The Hoop Dance includes dancers with hoops to show patterns in nature.
4–6. Answers will vary but may include that the Fancy Dance is fast and colorful. The Hoop Dance is the most difficult dance. Butterflies have peaceful lives.
7. Answers will vary.

Page 40

1. Answers will vary.
2. Answers will vary but should include two linking words (one in each sentence). 3. Answers will vary.

Page 41

1. B; 2. B; 3. F, T, T

Page 42

1–5. Answers will vary.

Page 43

1. A. clearly; B. swiftly; C. quickly; D. rapidly; 2. A. steep; B. blue; C. peaceful; D. huge; E. strong; F. angry

Page 44

1–4. Answers will vary.

Page 45

1–4. Answers will vary.

Page 46

1–4. Answers will vary.

Page 47

Answers will vary.

Page 48

Answers will vary.

Page 49

Answers will vary.

Page 50

1. family; 2. crew; 3. team; 4. staff; 5. band; 6. group; 7. army

Page 51

wolves, leaves, elves, shelves, scarves; echoes, heroes, tomatoes, potatoes, volcanoes

Page 52

1–6. Answers will vary.

Answer Key

Page 53

1. The snow boots were looked for by Tasha. 2. The large tree was climbed by Felipe. 3. The steak on the grill was cooked by Grandma. 4. At the kitchen table, Connor did his homework. 5. The ducks in the pond were counted by the girls.

Page 54

Groundhog Day; Canada Day; New Year's Day; Mother's Day

Mike and Henry's; Sabatino's Restaurant; Danny's Tea Shop; Yogurt Yummies; India; Tennessee; Japan; Atlantic

Page 55

A comma is needed after each greeting and closing.

Page 56

First present (tall, striped), Kate; second present (with flowers and bow), Kelly; third present (with flowers but without bow), Megan; fourth present (short, striped), Lisa 1. Rachel's; 2. Kate's; 3. brother's; 4. present's

Page 57

Answers will vary but may include sage, page, wage; edge, smudge, wedge; coil, foil, toil; boy, coy, Roy; phase, Phil, photo; knit, knot, know; lace, place, race; base, case, nose; gentle, germ, giraffe; Jack, Jenny, jump; gift, raft, rift; stuff, off, whiff.

Page 58

1.–4. lamp, lane, large, learn; 5.–8. lion, listen, lobster, locket; 9.–12. lot, loud, love, low

Page 59

1. B; 2. A; 3. C; 4. B; 5. A; 6. B; 7. C; 8. C

Page 60

1. landmark;
2. backward;
3. grandfather;
4. lighthouse;
5. copperhead;
6. cartwheels;
7. campground;
8. snowflakes;
9. stepladder;
10. hairstylist

Page 61

1. 2; 2. cuter, cutest; 3. noun; 4. 3; 5. to move fast; rush

Page 62

1–5. Answers will vary.

Page 63

1–5. Answers will vary. 6. big/huge; 7. chilly/freezing; 8. boiling/hot; 9. dusty/dirty; 10. stinking/smelly

Page 68

1. 18 worms; 2. 16 ears of corn; 3. 13 dogs; 4. 14 people; 5. 15 buttons; 6. 13 pencils

Page 69

1. 97 bulbs; 2. 88¢; 3. 93 peanuts; 4. 84¢; 5. 33 worms; 6. 62 candy bars

Page 70

1. 81 problems; 2. 29 problems; 3. 118 problems; 4. 8 students; 5. 64 papers; 6. 52 problems

Page 71

+	0	1	2	3	4	5	6	7	8	9	10
0	0	1	2	3	4	5	6	7	8	9	10
1	1	2	3	4	5	6	7	8	9	10	11
2	2	3	4	5	6	7	8	9	10	11	12
3	3	4	5	6	7	8	9	10	11	12	13
4	4	5	6	7	8	9	10	11	12	13	14
5	5	6	7	8	9	10	11	12	13	14	15
6	6	7	8	9	10	11	12	13	14	15	16
7	7	8	9	10	11	12	13	14	15	16	17
8	8	9	10	11	12	13	14	15	16	17	18
9	9	10	11	12	13	14	15	16	17	18	19
10	10	11	12	13	14	15	16	17	18	19	20

Page 72

1. $2 + 5 = 7$, $5 + 2 = 7$, $7 - 2 = 5$, $7 - 5 = 2$; 2. $8 + 2 = 10$; $2 + 8 = 10$, $10 - 2 = 8$, $10 - 8 = 2$; 3. $2 + 4 = 6$, $4 + 2 = 6$, $6 - 2 = 4$, $6 - 4 = 2$; 4. $8 + 3 = 11$, $3 + 8 = 11$, $11 - 8 = 3$, $11 - 3 = 8$; 5. $4 + 5 = 9$, $5 + 4 = 9$, $9 - 5 = 4$, $9 - 4 = 5$; 6. $6 + 3 = 9$, $3 + 6 = 9$, $9 - 3 = 6$, $9 - 6 = 3$

Page 73

1. 12, 3, 3, 10, 1, 2; 2. 5, 4, 8, 1, 1, 4; 3. 10, 10, 3, 5, 0, 5; 4. 3, 7, 2, 0, 5, 3; 5. 3, 9, 11, 4, 3, 6; 6. 2, 0, 0, 10, 10, 0

Page 74

1. 7, 6, 12, 0, 11, 7; 2. 14, 14, 0, 4, 13, 9; 3. 17, 6, 11, 7, 16, 4; 4. 9, 11, 2, 9, 3, 6; 5. 17, 5, 13, 9,

Answer Key

4, 10; 6. 2, 7, 11, 6, 6, 8

Page 75

1. 10, 11, 4, 6, 6, 12; 2. 7, 7, 1, 5, 11, 10; 3. 0, 2, 11, 9, 11, 8; 4. 10, 11, 9, 0, 4, 10; 5. 7, 12, 2, 12, 8, 4; 6. 7, 11, 7, 4, 9, 11; 7. 10, 12, 3, 12, 3, 7; 8. 9, 11, 5, 10, 2, 10; 9. 10, 3, 9, 4, 11, 5

Page 76

Even numbers: 2, 4, 6, 8, 10, 12, 14, 16, 18, 20, 22, 24, 26, 28, 30; Odd numbers: 1, 3, 5, 7, 9, 11, 13, 15, 17, 19, 21, 23, 25, 27, 29

Page 77

Even numbers: 2, 24, 20, 6, 12, 26, 28, 14, 8, 18, 22, 4, 16, 10, 30; Odd numbers: 3, 7, 29, 21, 13, 1, 25, 11, 17, 5, 23, 27, 19, 9, 15

Page 78

1. 20; 2. 24; 3. 12; 4. 50; 5. 12; 6. 30

Page 79

1. 1, 5, 4, 154; 2. 1, 6, 5, 165; 3. 2, 0, 7, 207; 4. 2, 8, 7, 287; 5. 3, 0, 8, 308; 6. 3, 3, 2, 332; 7. 3, 0, 0, 300; 8. 2, 8, 3, 283; 9. 0, 3, 3, 33

Page 80

1. 300, 2. 600; 3. 100; 4. 900; 5. 700; 6. 200; 7. 800; 8. 500; 9. 400

Page 81

1. 15, 30, 45; 2. 165, 180, 190, 195, 205, 210; 3. 320, 330, 360, 370, 390, 400; 4. 20, 30, 40, 60, 70, 80,

100, 110; 5. 455, 465, 475, 485, 495; 6. 300, 400, 700, 800; 7. 120, 125, 140, 145, 155, 160; 8. 650, 670, 690, 710, 730; 9. 235, 245, 255, 265, 275; 10. 200, 400, 500, 700, 900, 1000

Page 82

1. 15; 2. 20; 3. 35; 4. 40; 5. 10; 6. 80

Page 83

1. C; 2. G; 3. D; 4. H; 5. I; 6. J; 7. E; 8. A; 9. F; 10. B; 11. 313; 12. 809; 13. 426; 14. 211; 15. 751; 16. 105; 17. 532; 18. 944

Page 84

1. 533; 2. 947; 3. 755; 4. 479; 5. 21; 6. 102; 7. 506; 8. 98; 9. 609; 10. 698; 11. 400 + 50 + 6; 12. 300 + 20 + 4; 13. 100 + 50 + 2; 14. 500 + 60 + 9; 15. 400 + 30 + 1; 16. 20 + 2

Page 85

1. <; 2. <; 3. >; 4. >; 5. <; 6. =; 7. <; 8. <; 9. <; 10. =

Page 86

1. <; 2. >; 3. <; 4. >; 5. <; 6. <; 7. >; 8. <; 9. >; 10. <; 11. >; 12. <; 13. >; 14. <; 15. <; 16. <

Page 87

1. 35, 28, 53, 39, 39, 55, 55; 2. 29, 56, 96, 75, 85, 56, 18; 3. 69, 66, 97, 19, 39, 47, 90; 4. 28, 39, 100, 35, 92, 63, 89; 5. 35, 44, 35, 18, 47, 24, 25; 6. 11, 96, 99, 49, 99, 99, 39

Page 88

1. 3, 2; 2. 4, 1; 3. 6, 0; 4. 5, 7; 5. 29, 39, 8, 14, 15; 6. 25, 35, 26, 8, 18

Page 89

Across: B. 51; D. 19; E. 28; G. 24; I. 84; K. 32; L. 63; N. 21; P. 57; R. 41; S. 94; Down: A. 79; C. 12; D. 16; F. 86; H. 43; J. 46; M. 32; O. 14; Q. 79

Page 90

1. 156; 2. 84; 3. 192; 4. 107; 5. 129; 6. 127; 7. 124; 8. 155; 9. 106; 10. 128

Page 91

1. 318 cards; 2. 89 cards; 3. 22 pennies; 4. 216 bottle caps; 5. $119; 6. $45

Page 92

1. 595; 2. 211; 3. 496; 4. 242; 5. 214

Page 93

1. 33, 43, 53, 63, 73, 83; 2. 38, 48, 58, 68, 78, 88; 3. 46, 56, 66, 76, 86, 96, 106; 4. 369, 379, 389, 399, 409, 419, 429; 5. 815, 825, 835, 845, 855, 865, 875, 885; 6. 492, 592, 692, 792, 892, 992; 7. 319, 419, 519, 619, 719, 819, 919; 8. 288, 388, 488, 588, 688, 788, 888, 988; 9. 221, 321, 421, 521, 621, 721, 821, 921; 10. 252, 352, 452, 552, 652, 752, 852, 952

Page 94

1. 162, 152, 142, 132, 122, 112; 2. 689, 679, 669, 659, 649,

Answer Key

639; 3. 568, 558, 548, 538, 528, 518, 508;
4. 401, 391, 381, 371, 361, 351, 341; 5. 242,
232, 222, 212, 202, 192, 182, 172; 6. 603,
503, 403, 303, 203, 103; 7. 728, 628, 528,
428, 328, 228, 128; 8. 786, 686, 586, 486,
386, 286, 186; 9. 849, 749, 649, 549, 449,
349, 249, 149; 10. 805, 705, 605, 505, 405,
305, 205, 105

Page 95

1. 14 points, Explanations will vary. 2. 83
seashells, Explanations will vary. 3. 67
cars, Explanations will vary. 4. 81 bikes,
Explanations will vary.

Page 96

1. 6; 2. 2; 3. 3; 4. 5; 5. 2; 6. 4

Page 97

1. 3, 8; 2. 2, 5; 3. 6, 15; 4. 5, 13; 5. 1, 2; 6. 4,
10; 7. 5, 13; 8. 4, 10; 9. 2, 5

Page 98

1. less than 10 centimeters; 2. less than 5
meters; 3. less than 1 meter; 4. more than
1 centimeter; 5. more than 2 meters; 6.
more than 2 centimeters

Page 99

1. meter; 2. meter; 3. centimeter;
4. meter; 5. meter; 6. meter; 7.
centimeter; 8. meter; 9. centimeter

Page 100

A. 8; B. 11; C. 9; D. 3; E. 6; 1. 3 cm; 2. 6 cm;
3. 3 cm; 4. 2 cm; 5. 8 cm

Page 101

1. 32 in. 2. 3 in. 3. 7 cm − 4 cm = 3 cm; 4.
8 cm − 5 cm = 3 cm

Page 102

1. 18 in. 2. 78 in. 3. 25 in. 4. 25 cm; 5. 8 ft.
6. 83 cm

Page 103

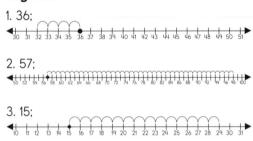

1. 36;

2. 57;

3. 15;

Page 104

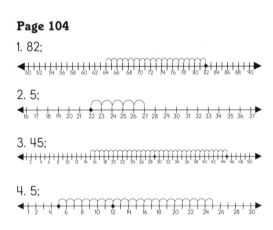

1. 82;

2. 5;

3. 45;

4. 5;

Page 105

1. 2:15; 2. 1:35; 3. 11:20; 4. 12:05; 5. 11:30; 6.
8:10; 7. 6:25; 8. 10:35; 9. 12:15; 10. 3:10; 11.
9:45; 12. 4:55

Page 106

Page 107

1. 8:15 or 15 minutes after 8 o'clock; 2.
1:40 or 40 minutes after 1 o'clock; 3. 11:20
or 20 minutes after 11 o'clock; 4. 4:35 or
35 minutes after 4 o'clock; 5. 9:05 or 5
minutes after 9 o'clock; 6. 12:45 or 45

Answer Key

minutes after 12 o'clock; 7. 6:55 or 55 minutes after 6 o'clock; 8. 2:30 or 30 minutes after 2 o'clock

Page 108

1. no, 60; 2. yes, 50; 3. yes, 95; 4. no, 29; 5. no, 80; 6. no, 49; 7. yes, 100; 8. no, 58

Page 109

1. $22.22; 2. $4.27; 3. $17.50; 4. $34.00; 5. $32.00; 6. $12.00

Page 110

1. 6 inches; 2. 1, 2, 3, 7, and 11 inches; 3. 5, 8, and 9 inches; 4. 2; 5. 2; 6. 4 inches

Page 111

1. 11; 2. Luis; 3. Justin; 4. Penny; 5. 20

Page 112

Type of Frozen Treat					
Grape	🥤	🥤	🥤		
Orange	🥤	🥤	🥤		
Cranberry	🥤	🥤			
Cherry	🥤	🥤	🥤	🥤	
Strawberry	🥤	🥤	🥤	🥤	🥤
Kiwi	🥤	🥤	🥤		
Apple	🥤				

Number of Frozen Fruit Treats Eaten

Page 113

1–8. Answers will vary.

Page 114

1. quadrilateral; 2. triangle; 3. triangle; 4. pentagon; 5. quadrilateral; 6. triangle; 7. pentagon; 8. pentagon; 9. quadrilateral; 10. triangle; 11. quadrilateral; 12. pentagon

Page 115

1. square, rectangle, rhombus, and trapezoid; 2. square; 3. triangle; 4. circle; 5. pentagon; 6. hexagon; 7. octagon; 8. A rectangle has four sides. The four sides of a square are the same length.

Page 116

Answers will vary but may include:

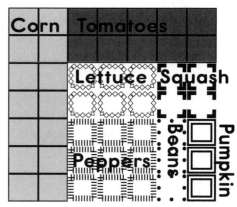

Page 117

1. 2: 1 × 10 and 2 × 5; 2. 3: 1 × 12, 3 × 4, and 2 × 6; 3. 2: 1 × 15 and 3 × 5; 4. 3: 1 × 18, 3 × 6, and 2 × 9; 5. 3: 1 × 20, 2 × 10, and 4 × 5

Page 118

1. 1; 2. 1; 3. 3; 4. 3; 5. 2; 6. 1

Page 119

1. $\frac{1}{4}$ 2. $\frac{1}{2}$; 3. $\frac{2}{4}$; 4. $\frac{3}{4}$; 5. $\frac{2}{3}$; 6. $\frac{1}{3}$

Page 120

1–6. Answers will vary but may include:

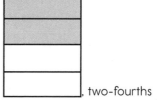

Answer Key

3.
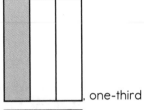
, one-third

4.
, three-fourths

4.
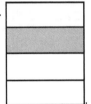
, three-fourths

5.
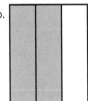
, one-fourth

5.
, one-fourth

6.
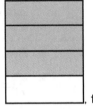
, two-thirds

6.
, two-thirds

Page 121

1–6. Answers will vary but may include:

1.

, one-half

2.

, two-fourths

3.

, one-third

Which word has a long vowel sound?

flush

help

nose

ship

Which word has a short vowel sound?

cave

fang

glide

load

Which word has a long vowel sound?

path

rake

shop

this

Which two vowel letters complete the word that means "come together"?

m __ __ t

Which word has a short vowel sound?

cave

fang

glide

load

Which word has a long vowel sound?

flush

help

nose

ship

Which two vowel letters complete the word that means "come together"?

m _e_ _e_ t

Which word has a long vowel sound?

path

rake

shop

this

Which two vowel letters complete the word that means "a strong cord"?

r __ p __

Which two vowel letters complete the word that means "a bad feeling"?

p __ __ n

Which word means "next to"?

beneath

beside

beyond

Which word means "the main part of a country"?

mainly

landscape

mainland

Which two vowel letters complete the word that means "a bad feeling"?

p _a_ _i_ n

Which two vowel letters complete the word that means "a strong cord"?

r _o_ p _e_

Which word means "the main part of a country"?

mainly

landscape

mainland

Which word means "next to"?

beneath

beside

beyond

Which prefix can be added to make a word that means "take apart"?

re-   un-   pre-

_____do

Which suffix can be added to make a word that means "full of forgetting"?

-less   -ing   -ful

forget_____

Which word is spelled correctly?

furst

frst

first

Which word is spelled correctly?

straight

strate

straite

Which suffix can be added to make a word that means "full of forgetting"?

-less   -ing   -ful

forgetful

Which prefix can be added to make a word that means "take apart"?

re-   un-   pre-

undo

Which word is spelled correctly?

straight

strate

straite

Which word is spelled correctly?

furst

frst

first

Which collective noun completes the sentence?

A _____ of birds swooped over the lake.

herd
flock
tribe

Which collective noun completes the sentence?

Did the _____ applaud at the end of the show?

audience
crew
team

What word means "more than one woman"?

What word means "more than one goose"?

Which collective noun completes the sentence?

Did the <u>audience</u> applaud at the end of the show?

audience
crew
team

Which collective noun completes the sentence?

A __<u>flock</u>__ of birds swooped over the lake.

herd
flock
tribe

What word means "more than one goose"?

geese

What word means "more than one woman"?

women

What word means "more than one mouse"?

Use the word parts to form two reflexive pronouns.

my   selves

our   self

What reflexive pronoun completes the sentence?

Tasha decided to make the costume

_____.

Complete the second sentence with a verb in the past tense.

I like to give my dog treats. Yesterday, I _____ her two treats.

Use the word parts to form two reflexive pronouns.

myself, ourselves

What word means "more than one mouse"?

mice

Complete the second sentence with a verb in the past tense.

I like to give my dog treats. Yesterday, I __gave__ her two treats.

What reflexive pronoun completes the sentence?

Tasha decided to make the costume ____herself____.

Give the past-tense form of each verb.

hold

put

think

Complete the second sentence with a verb in the past tense.

I will write a new story this week. Last week, I _____ a mystery story.

Which word is an adjective?

quickly

yellow

umbrella

them

Which word is an adverb?

tall

am

easily

sister

Complete the second sentence with a verb in the past tense.

I will write a new story this week. Last week, I __wrote__ a mystery story.

Give the past-tense form of each verb.

held

put

thought

Which word is an adverb?

tall

am

easily

sister

Which word is an adjective?

quickly

yellow

umbrella

them

Use the words to complete the sentence.

warmly   cold

It is a _____ day, so be sure to dress _____.

How are the two sentences different?

I played a game today.

I played a new game earlier today.

How are the two sentences different?

Dad took the dog for a walk.

The dog was walked by Dad.

How are the two sentences different?

We ate popcorn at the fair, and we saw rabbits.

We saw rabbits at the fair, and we ate popcorn.

How are the two sentences different?

The second sentence has the adjective *new* and the adverb *earlier*.

Use the words to complete the sentence.

warmly   cold

It is a __cold__ day, so be sure to dress __warmly__.

How are the two sentences different?

The two parts of the compound sentence are in a different order.

How are the two sentences different?

The subject of the first sentence is *Dad*. The subject of the second sentence is *The dog*.

Which words should begin with a capital letter?

Our class will have a party on valentine's day.

Which words should begin with a capital letter?

We ate lunch at doodle deli.

Which words should begin with a capital letter?

Have you ever been to chicago, illinois?

In which position does a comma belong?

Dear ☐ Aunt ☐ Leslie ☐

Which words should begin with a capital letter?

We ate lunch at Doodle Deli.

Which words should begin with a capital letter?

Our class will have a party on Valentine's Day.

In which position does a comma belong?

Dear Aunt Leslie,

Which words should begin with a capital letter?

Have you ever been to Chicago, Illinois?

In which position does a comma belong?

With A **love** B **Langston** C

Which is the correct contraction for *will not*?

A. w'ont

B. wont

C. won't

D. wo'nt

Which is the correct contraction for *she will*?

A. shell

B. sh'ell

C. shel'l

D. she'll

Which is the correct way to write "the lunch belonging to Bella"?

A. Bellas lunch

B. Bella's lunch

C. Bellases lunch

D. Bellas' lunch

Which is the correct contraction for *will not*?

A. w'ont

B. wont

(C.) won't

D. wo'nt

In which position does a comma belong?

With love,
Langston

Which is the correct way to write "the lunch belonging to Bella"?

A. Bellas lunch

(B.) Bella's lunch

C. Bellases lunch

D. Bellas' lunch

Which is the correct contraction for *she will*?

A. shell

B. sh'ell

C. shel'l

(D.) she'll

Which is the correct way to write "the jacket belonging to Marc"?

A. Marc's jacket

B. Marcs jacket

C. Marcs' jacket

D. Marces jacket

You could use the spelling pattern found in *bean* to help you spell which word?

A. been

B. best

C. spear

D. side

You could use the spelling pattern found in *total* to help you spell which word?

A. local

B. took

C. loan

D. tell

You could use the spelling pattern found in *bird* to help you spell which word?

A. bang

B. shirt

C. soft

D. badly

You could use the spelling pattern found in *bean* to help you spell which word?

A. been

B. best

C. spear

D. side

Which is the correct way to write "the jacket belonging to Marc"?

A. Marc's jacket

B. Marcs jacket

C. Marcs' jacket

D. Marces jacket

You could use the spelling pattern found in *bird* to help you spell which word?

A. bang

B. shirt

C. soft

D. badly

You could use the spelling pattern found in *total* to help you spell which word?

A. local

B. took

C. loan

D. tell

Which would be the best way to say hello to your principal?

A. Hey!

B. Good morning.

C. How's it going?

Which sentence is correct?

A. I didn't see nothing.

B. I did not see nothing.

C. I did not see anything.

Which would be the best way to say good-bye to a good friend?

A. It was a pleasure to see you.

B. See ya later.

C. We must get together again soon.

What does *gaze* mean in the sentence?

Gaze to your left to see the famous bridge.

A. walk

B. turn

C. look

Which sentence is correct?

A. I didn't see nothing.

B. I did not see nothing.

C. I did not see anything.

Which would be the best way to say hello to your principal?

A. Hey!

B. Good morning.

C. How's it going?

What does *gaze* mean in the sentence?

Gaze to your left to see the famous bridge.

A. walk

B. turn

C. look

Which would be the best way to say good-bye to a good friend?

A. It was a pleasure to see you.

B. See ya later.

C. We must get together again soon.

What does *attention* mean in the sentence?

Give me your attention when I explain the directions.

A. ability to pay

B. careful thought

C. being awake

What does *discarded* mean in the sentence?

Agnes opened her banana and discarded the peel.

A. threw away

B. ate

C. created

The word *heat* means "to warm up." What does *reheat* mean?

The word *even* means "equal or fair." What does *uneven* mean?

What does *discarded* mean in the sentence?

Agnes opened her banana and discarded the peel.

A. threw away

B. ate

C. created

What does *attention* mean in the sentence?

Give me your attention when I explain the directions.

A. ability to pay

B. careful thought

C. being awake

The word *even* means "equal or fair." What does *uneven* mean?

not equal or fair

The word *heat* means "to warm up." What does *reheat* mean?

to warm up again

The word *connect* means "to put together." What does *disconnect* mean?

Which has the root word *add*?

allow

addition

actually

Which has the root word *begin*?

start

being

beginning

Which has the root word *act*?

actor

test

play

Which has the root word *add*?

allow

actually

The word *connect* means "to put together." What does *disconnect* mean?

to take apart

Which has the root word *act*?

actor

test

play

Which has the root word *begin*?

start

being

beginning

Combine the words in different ways to make two compound words.

night

flash

light

Combine the words in different ways to make two compound words.

dog

boat

house

Combine the words in different ways to make two compound words.

shelf

book

note

Which can be added to *ring* to make a compound word?

bell

hand

ear

Combine the words in different ways to make two compound words.

doghouse, houseboat

Combine the words in different ways to make two compound words.

nightlight, flashlight

Which can be added to *ring* to make a compound word?

bell

hand

ear

earring

Combine the words in different ways to make two compound words.

bookshelf, notebook

Which can be added to *pepper* to make a compound word?

salt

spicy

mint

Which can be added to *boy* to make a compound word?

cow

girl

little

Which are sticky?

jelly

shampoo

milk

gum

Which are fragrant?

roses

blankets

soup

stories

Which can be added to *boy* to make a compound word?

(cow)

girl

little

cowboy

© Carson-Dellosa

Which can be added to *pepper* to make a compound word?

salt

spicy

(mint)

peppermint

© Carson-Dellosa

Which are fragrant?

(roses)

blankets

(soup)

stories

© Carson-Dellosa

Which are sticky?

(jelly)

shampoo

milk

(gum)

© Carson-Dellosa

Which are colorful?

ponies

butterflies

cartoons

sandboxes

Which word belongs: *stare*, *look*, *search*, _____.

A. find

B. peek

C. tap

D. touch

Which word belongs: *nibble*, *taste*, *bite*, _____.

A. chomp

B. lick

C. smell

D. poke

Which word belongs: *chilly*, *cold*, *frosty*, _____.

A. toasty

B. snow

C. freezing

D. warmth

Which word belongs:
stare, *look*, *search*,

_____.

A. find

(B.) peek

C. tap

D. touch

Which are colorful?

ponies

butterflies

cartoons

sandboxes

Which word belongs:
chilly, *cold*, *frosty*,

_____.

A. toasty

B. snow

(C.) freezing

D. warmth

Which word belongs:
nibble, *taste*, *bite*,

_____.

(A.) chomp

B. lick

C. smell

D. poke

8 students are on the rug. 16 students are working at tables. 5 students are meeting with Ms. Bailey. How many students are in the classroom?

Tell whether the next number in each pattern will be odd or even.

2, 4, 8, 16, ___

3, 4, 5, 6, ___

Add to find the total number of flowers.

Solve mentally.

20 – 7 = ?

12 – 8 = ?

18 – 4 = ?

9 – 3 = ?

Tell whether the next number in each pattern will be odd or even.

2, 4, 8, 16, <u>32</u>

even

3, 4, 5, 6, <u>7</u>

odd

8 students are on the rug. 16 students are working at tables. 5 students are meeting with Ms. Bailey. How many students are in the classroom?

29 students

Solve mentally.

20 – 7 = 13

12 – 8 = 4

18 – 4 = 14

9 – 3 = 6

Add to find the total number of flowers.

3 + 3 + 3 = 9

Which equation shows the number of dots?

●●●●
●●●●
●●●●

A. $9 + 2 = ?$

B. $6 + 6 = ?$

C. $10 + 3 = ?$

D. $4 + 6 = ?$

While playing a video game, Misha found 54 gold coins in one room, 76 silver coins in another room, and 16 gold coins in a third room. How many gold coins did Misha find?

Solve mentally.

$8 + 7 = ?$

$4 + 6 = ?$

$3 + 9 = ?$

$5 + 9 = ?$

Solve mentally.

$9 + 7 = ?$

$5 + 8 = ?$

$2 + 6 = ?$

$4 + 7 = ?$

While playing a video game, Misha found 54 gold coins in one room, 76 silver coins in another room, and 16 gold coins in a third room. How many gold coins did Misha find?

70 gold coins

Which equation shows the number of dots?

●●●●
●●●●
●●●●

A. $9 + 2 = ?$

(B.) $6 + 6 = ?$

C. $10 + 3 = ?$

D. $4 + 6 = ?$

Solve mentally.

$9 + 7 = 16$

$5 + 8 = 13$

$2 + 6 = 8$

$4 + 7 = 11$

Solve mentally.

$8 + 7 = 15$

$4 + 6 = 10$

$3 + 9 = 12$

$5 + 9 = 14$

Which number could be added to 7 to get an even number?

2

4

6

7

How many? Count by twos.

Which equation shows the total number?

A. 3 + 4 + 4 = ?

B. 4 + 4 + 4 = ?

C. 3 + 3 + 3 = ?

D. 4 + 3 + 4 = ?

Sophie had 90 minutes to play outside. She roller-skated for 19 minutes. She did cartwheels for 8 minutes. She played tag for 22 minutes. How many minutes did she have left to play?

How many? Count by twos.

12

Which number could be added to 7 to get an even number?

2

4

6

(7)

Sophie had 90 minutes to play outside. She roller-skated for 19 minutes. She did cartwheels for 8 minutes. She played tag for 22 minutes. How many minutes did she have left to play?

41 minutes

Which equation shows the total number?

A. 3 + 4 + 4 = ?

(B.) 4 + 4 + 4 = ?

C. 3 + 3 + 3 = ?

D. 4 + 3 + 4 = ?

Solve mentally.

20 – 15 = ?

14 + 3 = ?

16 + 2 = ?

19 – 6 = ?

Which shows 10 + 10?

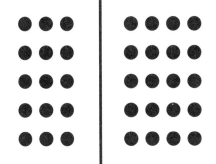

Which equation shows the total number?

A. 6 + 6 + 6 = ?

B. 3 + 3 + 3 = ?

C. 6 + 6 + 3 = ?

D. 3 + 3 + 6 = ?

Ben decorated 48 holiday cookies. He gave 15 to the kids at his bus stop. He gave 12 to his teacher. How many cookies did Ben have left?

Which shows 10 + 10?

Solve mentally.

$$20 - 15 = 5$$

$$14 + 3 = 17$$

$$16 + 2 = 18$$

$$19 - 6 = 13$$

Ben decorated 48 holiday cookies. He gave 15 to the kids at his bus stop. He gave 12 to his teacher. How many cookies did Ben have left?

21 cookies

Which equation shows the total number?

A. 6 + 6 + 6 = ?

B. 3 + 3 + 3 = ?

C. 6 + 6 + 3 = ?

D. 3 + 3 + 6 = ?

Count by tens to 500.

310, 320, 330...

How many hundreds?

600

Give the number.

800 + 70 + 4

Compare using <, >, or =.

397 ◯ 379

How many hundreds?

600
6 hundreds

Count by tens to 500.

310, 320, 330...

340, 350, 360,
370, 380, 390,
400, 410, 420,
430, 440, 450,
460, 470, 480,
490, 500

Compare using <, >, or =.

397 > 379

Give the number.

800 + 70 + 4
874

Add.

$$36$$
$$+ \; 46$$

Use place value to help you add.

hundreds tens ones

$$5 \; 6 \; 2$$
$$+ \; 1 \; 4 \; 7$$

Count by hundreds to 900.

200, 300, 400...

Add mentally.

$$362 + 100 =$$

Use place value to help you add.

hundreds tens ones

$$
\begin{array}{r}
5\;6\;2 \\
+\;1\;4\;7 \\
\hline
709
\end{array}
$$

Add.

$$
\begin{array}{r}
36 \\
+\;46 \\
\hline
82
\end{array}
$$

Add mentally.

$$362 + 100 = 462$$

Count by hundreds to 900.

200, 300, 400…

500, 600, 700, 800, 900

Add.

$$
\begin{array}{r}
12 \\
22 \\
31 \\
+\ 18 \\
\hline
\end{array}
$$

How many hundreds?

400

Subtract.

$$
\begin{array}{r}
751 \\
-\ 582 \\
\hline
\end{array}
$$

Compare using <, >, or =.

989 $\bigcirc$ 900 + 90 + 8

How many hundreds?

400

4 hundreds

Add.

$$
\begin{array}{r}
12 \\
22 \\
31 \\
+\ 18 \\
\hline
83
\end{array}
$$

Compare using <, >, or =.

989 $<$ 900 + 90 + 8

Subtract.

$$
\begin{array}{r}
751 \\
-\ 582 \\
\hline
169
\end{array}
$$

Subtract mentally.

765 – 10 =

Use place value to help you subtract.

hundreds tens ones

$$\begin{array}{r} 5\,0\,0 \\ -\,2\,6\,4 \\ \hline \end{array}$$

Add.

$$\begin{array}{r} 24 \\ 37 \\ 18 \\ +\,26 \\ \hline \end{array}$$

Give the number.

400 + 90 + 4 =

Math
2.NBT.B.7

Use place value to help you subtract.

hundreds tens ones

$$\begin{array}{r} 500 \\ -\ 264 \\ \hline 236 \end{array}$$

Math
2.NBT.B.8

Subtract mentally.

$$765 - 10 = 755$$

Math
2.NBT.A.3

Give the number.

$$400 + 90 + 4 =$$

494

Math
2.NBT.B.6

Add.

$$\begin{array}{r} 24 \\ 37 \\ 18 \\ +\ 26 \\ \hline 105 \end{array}$$

Measure in inches and centimeters.

_____ in. _____ cm

Use the number line to add.

18 + 6

If you have 2 quarters, 3 nickels, and 4 pennies, how many cents do you have?

Which is the best estimate for the length of a toothbrush?

A. 2 inches

B. 6 inches

C. 12 inches

D. 20 inches

Use the number line to add.

18 + 6

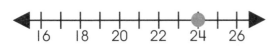

Measure in inches and centimeters.

__2__ in. __5__ cm

Which is the best estimate for the length of a toothbrush?

A. 2 inches

B. 6 inches

C. 12 inches

D. 20 inches

If you have 2 quarters, 3 nickels, and 4 pennies, how many cents do you have?

69¢

Measure in centimeters. How much longer is the chocolate bar than the peppermint?

How many more birds came to the feeder on Monday than on Thursday?

 = 5 birds

Which is the best unit to use for measuring the distance between the slide and the monkey bars on a playground?

A. centimeter

B. meter

Tell the time.

How many more birds came to the feeder on Monday than on Thursday?

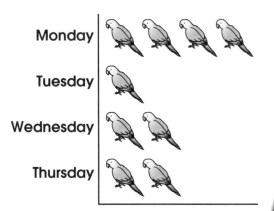

Monday
Tuesday
Wednesday
Thursday

10 birds

Measure in centimeters. How much longer is the chocolate bar than the peppermint?

CHOCOLATE

3 centimeters longer

Tell the time.

6:10

Which is the best unit to use for measuring the distance between the slide and the monkey bars on a playground?

A. centimeter

B. meter

Use the number line to subtract.

100 − 40 =

Measure in inches. How much longer is the magnifying glass?

Allie is 51 inches tall. Her dad is 73 inches tall. How much taller is Allie's dad than Allie?

Tell the time.

Measure in inches. How much longer is the magnifying glass?

$\frac{1}{2}$ in. longer

Use the number line to subtract.

100 – 40 =

Tell the time.

2:55

Allie is 51 inches tall. Her dad is 73 inches tall. How much taller is Allie's dad than Allie?

22 in.

In his piggy bank, Oliver found 3 dollar bills, 6 quarters, three dimes, one nickel, and 18 pennies. How much money does he have?

On Monday, 35 children chose a sandwich for lunch. How many pictures should be added to the graph for Monday?

Monday
Tuesday
Wednesday
Thursday

= 10 sandwiches

Measure in inches and centimeters.

_____ in. _____ cm

A door is 89 inches away from Martin. Martin's remote-control car drove a distance of 42 inches. How much farther does the car need to drive to reach the doorway?

On Monday, 35 children chose a sandwich for lunch. How many pictures should be added to the graph for Monday?

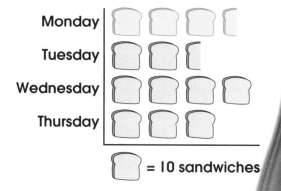

Monday
Tuesday
Wednesday
Thursday

= 10 sandwiches

In his piggy bank, Oliver found 3 dollar bills, 6 quarters, three dimes, one nickel, and 18 pennies. How much money does he have?

$5.03

A door is 89 inches away from Martin. Martin's remote-control car drove a distance of 42 inches. How much farther does the car need to drive to reach the doorway?

47 inches

Measure in inches and centimeters.

$1\frac{1}{2}$ in. 4 cm

Name the shape.

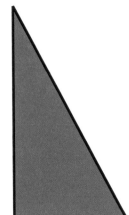

Name the shape.

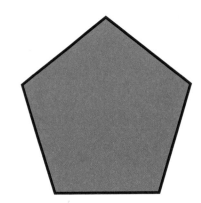

Name the shape.

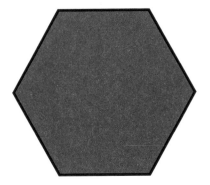

Name the shape.

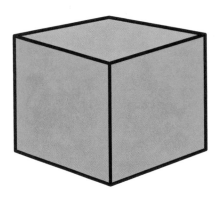

Name the shape.

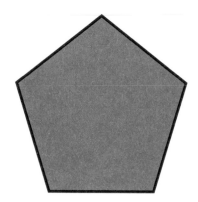

pentagon

Name the shape.

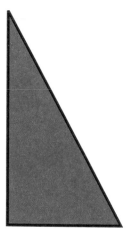

triangle

Name the shape.

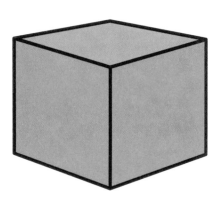

cube

Name the shape.

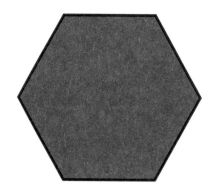

hexagon

Which is a quadrilateral?

A.

B.

Which shape has 6 faces?

A. cylinder

B. sphere

C. pyramid

D. cube

How many squares?

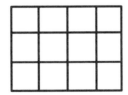

How many squares?

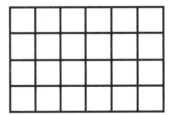

Which shape has 6 faces?

A. cylinder

B. sphere

C. pyramid

D. cube

Which is a quadrilateral?

A.

B.

How many squares?

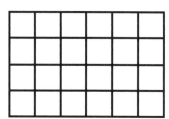

24

How many squares?

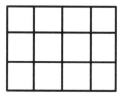

12

How many halves are shaded?

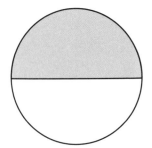

How many halves are shaded?

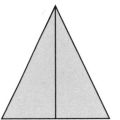

How many thirds are shaded?

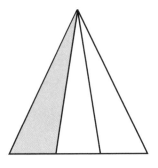

How many thirds are shaded?

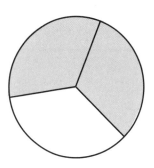

How many halves are shaded?

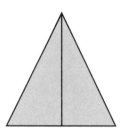

2 halves

How many halves are shaded?

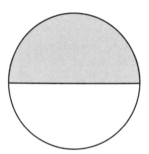

I half

How many thirds are shaded?

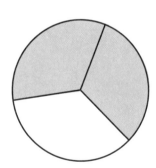

2 thirds

How many thirds are shaded?

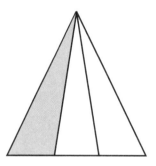

I third

How many thirds are shaded?

How many fourths are shaded?

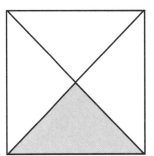

How many fourths are shaded?

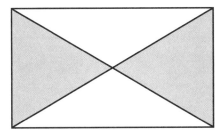

How many fourths are shaded?

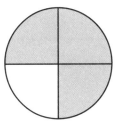

How many fourths are shaded?

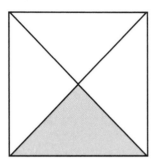

I fourth

How many thirds are shaded?

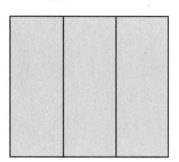

3 thirds

How many fourths are shaded?

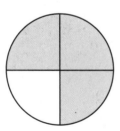

3 fourths

How many fourths are shaded?

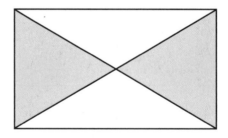

2 fourths